Already published in the series (*continued*):

THACKERAY: VANITY FAIR

by

ROBIN GILMOUR

Lecturer in English,
University of Aberdeen

EDWARD ARNOLD

First published 1982 by
Edward Arnold (Publishers) Ltd
4I Bedford Square,
London WC1B 3DQ

British Library Cataloguing in Publication Data

Gilmour, Robin
   Thackeray, Vanity fair. — (Studies in English
   literature)
   1. Thackeray, William Makepeace. Vanity fair
   I. Title   II. Series
   823′ .8   PR5618

   ISBN 0-7131-6321-6

For Susie, Lucy, Jonathan and Richard

Printed in Great Britain by
The Camelot Press Ltd, Southampton

General Preface

The object of this series is to provide studies of individual novels, plays and groups of poems and essays which are known to be widely read by students. The emphasis is on clarification and evaluation; biographical and historical facts, while they may be discussed when they throw light on particular elements in a writer's work, are generally subordinated to critical discussion. What kind of work is this? What exactly goes on here? How good is this work, and why? These are the questions that each writer will try to answer.

It should be emphasized that these studies are written on the assumption that the reader has already read carefully the work discussed. The objective is not to enable students to deliver opinions about works they have not read, nor is it to provide ready-made ideas to be applied to works that have been read. In one sense all critical interpretation can be regarded as foisting opinions on readers, but to accept this is to deny the advantages of any sort of critical discussion directed at students or indeed at anybody else. The aim of these studies is to provide what Coleridge called in another context 'aids to reflection' about the works discussed. The interpretations are offered as suggestive rather than as definitive, in the hope of stimulating the reader into developing further his own insights. This is after all the function of all critical discourse among sensible people.

Because of the interest which this kind of study has aroused, it has been decided to extend it first from merely English literature to include also some selected works of American literature and now further to include selected works in English by Commonwealth writers. The criterion will remain that the book studied is important in itself and is widely read by students.

DAVID DAICHES

A Note on the Text and Serialization

All references to *Vanity Fair* are by chapter number to the standard edition of the novel, edited by Geoffrey and Kathleen Tillotson (London: Methuen, 1963). This edition is available in the American 'Riverside' series (Boston: Houghton Mifflin, 1963), although it is not at present in print in the United Kingdom. The Penguin edition, edited by J. I. M. Stewart (London: 1968), has the same chapter numbering as the 'Riverside' edition.

In common with many other classic Victorian novels, *Vanity Fair* was serialized in twenty monthly parts or numbers from January 1847 to July 1848 (the last a double number). Both the Tillotson and the Penguin editions indicate the serial divisions, but as I shall be referring to them in the course of this study it may be helpful to have them set out at the start:

Date	Number	Chapters
January 1847	I	1–4
February	II	5–7
March	III	8–11
April	IV	12–14
May	V	15–18
June	VI	19–22
July	VII	23–5
August	VIII	26–9
September	IX	30–2
October	X	33–5
November	XI	36–8
December	XII	39–42
January 1848	XIII	43–6
February	XIV	47–50
March	XV	51–3
April	XVI	54–6
May	XVII	57–60
June	XVIII	61–3
July	XIX–XX	64–7

Contents

Preface: 'Before the Curtain'

Thackeray's original title for his book, before he hit on *Vanity Fair*, was 'A Novel without a Hero', and this appeared as the subtitle when the novel was published as a single volume in 1848. Both title and subtitle are pointers to the kind of novel this is. 'A Novel without a Hero' suggests what every reader soon discovers for himself, that this is not a story built around a central character (like Fielding's *Tom Jones* or Dickens's *David Copperfield*) but a study of the interweaving destinies of a number of characters, none of whom is allowed to dominate, and of the society they inhabit. It also implies a sceptical attitude towards conventional notions of heroism and the heroic, significant in a novel which is to have the battle of Waterloo at the heart of its action and structure. Indeed, in many ways *Vanity Fair* can be seen as the English *War and Peace* with the battle scenes left out − a comparison which will be explored further in my second chapter. Both works deal with love and marriage against the background of the Napoleonic Wars, but Thackeray differs from Tolstoy in his oblique and irreverent treatment of battle itself; he is less concerned with the stirring events of war than with its effects on those, like Amelia, who have to pick up the pieces afterwards. 'We do not claim to rank among the military novelists', the narrator remarks on the threshold of Waterloo. 'Our place is with the non-combatants. When the decks are cleared for action we go below and wait meekly' (ch. 30). Here, as in the subtitle, Thackeray is at pains to remind us of the kind of novel he is *not* writing, the possibilities for military heroics he is forgoing. This is to be a book which will disappoint the habitual attitudes and expectations of novel-readers, and do so deliberately, in the interests of a deeper truthfulness.

What of the title itself? 'Vanity Fair' was a brilliant choice, as Thackeray realized; it came to him in the middle of the night and, he said, 'I jumped out of bed and ran three times round my room, uttering as I went, "Vanity Fair, Vanity Fair, Vanity Fair" '.[1] His delight is understandable: 'Vanity Fair' was just the sort of generalizing title needed to

[1] See Gordon N. Ray, *Thackeray: the Uses of Adversity* (London: Oxford University Press, 1955), p. 385.

underline the predominantly social focus of the 'Novel without a Hero', while at the same time tapping the moral associations of the great Puritan classic from which it comes, *The Pilgrim's Progress*. Thackeray's first readers were more intimate with Bunyan than most of us are likely to be today, so it may be helpful to see what Vanity Fair meant in its original context. Here is Bunyan's description of the Fair:

> Almost five thousand years agone, there were Pilgrims walking to the Celestial City, as these two honest persons are; and *Beelzebub*, *Apollyon*, and *Legion*, with their Companions, perceiving by the path that the Pilgrims made that their way to the City lay through *this Town* of *Vanity*, they contrived here to set up a Fair; a Fair wherein should be sold of *all sorts of Vanity*, and that it should last all the year long. Therefore at *this Fair* are all such Merchandize sold, as Houses, Lands, Trades, Places, Honours, Preferments, Titles, Countries, Kingdoms, Lusts, Pleasures, and Delights of all sorts, as Whores, Bawds, Wives, Husbands, Children, Masters, Servants, Lives, Blood, Bodies, Souls, Silver, Gold, Pearls, Precious Stones, and what not.[2]

Bunyan had in mind the London of his time, although the image of the Fair can apply to any large city or centre. For Thackeray it is the 'world', upper- and middle-class society with its basis in London, and more particularly the fashionable inhabitants of Mayfair. And it is not hard to see – especially in that remarkable last sentence – the appropriateness of Bunyan's Fair to Thackeray's vision of his own society. The long catalogue of 'Merchandize' for sale powerfully evokes the bustling life and moral confusion of the place. Bunyan's juxtapositions are striking: we expect 'Houses', 'Preferments' and 'Pleasures' to be sold in Vanity Fair, but by bringing 'Whores' and 'Bawds' into conjunction with 'Wives, Husbands, Children', and 'Souls' with 'Silver, Gold', he makes us feel how the corrupting power of money has invaded the most natural and intimate areas of life, reducing all to 'Merchandize'. In Thackeray's vision, too, money weighs more than love or loyalty for most of his characters; it can buy social acceptability for the parvenu, and toadying attentions for the unlovable; the loss of it can rupture friendship and lead, as Amelia discovers, to cruel ostracism and the slow poisoning of a once happy home. ' "I think I could be a good woman if I had five thousand a

[2] *The Pilgrim's Progress* (Oxford: Clarendon Press, 1960), p. 88.

year" ' (ch. 41), Becky reflects, and her career demonstrates the extent to which respectability depends upon a solid income.

The pressure of money is felt everywhere in *Vanity Fair* and none of the characters can escape it; in this respect the Fair, the 'world', is more powerful than the individuals who compose it. To quote again from *The Pilgrim's Progress*: 'Now, as I said, the way to the Celestial City lyes just thorow *this Town*, where this lusty Fair is kept; and he that will go to the City, and yet not go thorow this Town, must needs *go out of the World*' (p. 89). For Thackeray, as for Bunyan, Vanity Fair is inescapable; one cannot live in the world and not pass through it. The difference is that Bunyan's pilgrims are indeed passing through, on their way to the Celestial City beyond. For Thackeray and his characters there seems to be no Celestial City. 'What I want', he wrote to his mother while at work on the novel, 'is to make a set of people living without God in the world (only that is a cant phrase) greedy pompous mean perfectly self-satisfied for the most part and at ease about their superior virtue'.[3] Vanity Fair *is* the world, and however much Thackeray's narrator may castigate its greed and hypocrisy and moral blindness, he can no more escape it than its inhabitants can. As Emerson observed, 'Thackeray's *Vanity Fair* is pathetic in its name, and in his use of the name; an admission it is from a man of fashion in the London of 1850 that poor old Puritan Bunyan was right in his perception of the London of 1650. And yet now in Thackeray is the added wisdom, or skepticism, that, though this be really so, he must yet live in tolerance of, and practically in homage and obedience to, these illusions'.[4] Thackeray satirizes Vanity Fair but he also accepts it, and this alternation of satirical indignation and world-weary tolerance partly accounts for that shifting ambivalence of tone which is his distinctive 'signature'.

We are introduced to the Fair, and also to the unsettling quality of Thackeray's narrative tone, in 'Before the Curtain', the preface he added to the completed novel for its publication in book form. Here he comes

[3] *The Letters and Private Papers of William Makepeace Thackeray*, ed. Gordon N. Ray (4 vols., London: Oxford University Press, 1945–6) II, p. 309; letter of 2 July 1847.

[4] Quoted by Gordon N. Ray, '*Vanity Fair*: One Version of the Novelist's Responsibility', *Essays by Divers Hands*, New Series XXV (1950), pp. 87–101; reprinted in Austin Wright, ed., *Victorian Literature: Modern Essays in Criticism* (New York: Oxford University Press, 1961), p. 355.

forward in one of his many narrative guises, that of the 'Manager of the Performance', presenter of a puppet-show in one of the booths in Vanity Fair. A certain sad detachment is the keynote of this preface, linking it with the cry of *Vanitas Vanitatum* in the closing words of the novel. As he walks through the Fair the Manager observes the noise and activity, yet 'a feeling of profound melancholy comes over him in his survey of the bustling place'. Then in the third paragraph he invites the reader to come in:

> Some people consider Fairs immoral altogether, and eschew such, with their servants and families: very likely they are right. But persons who think otherwise, and are of a lazy, or a benevolent, or a sarcastic mood, may perhaps like to step in for half an hour, and look at the performances. There are scenes of all sorts; some dreadful combats, some grand and lofty horse-riding, some scenes of high life, and some of very middling indeed; some love-making for the sentimental, and some light comic business; the whole accompanied by appropriate scenery, and brilliantly illuminated with the Author's own candles.

There is, surely, something just a little disquieting about this passage. Partly it is the narrator's careless, take-it-or-leave-it attitude to his story. He seems to disparage his own art and belittle his achievement in the body of the novel by presenting it as a prospectus for a fairground 'performance' ('some love-making for the sentimental, and some light comic business'). This is of a piece with his reference in the next paragraph to his characters as 'puppets' – 'the famous little Becky Puppet', 'the Amelia Doll' – wilfully denying them (or so it seems) the autonomous life we may find in them as we read. Then there are his apparently low expectations of his audience: the story will appeal to 'persons . . . of a lazy, or a benevolent, or a sarcastic mood'. Where does this leave the ordinary reader who is neither lazy nor sarcastic, and who may have been genuinely moved by the power and credibility of Thackeray's art?

The answer might be – unsettled. The Victorian critic Walter Bagehot described Thackeray as an 'uncomfortable writer' and noted, perceptively, the 'peculiar and characteristic scepticism' which marked his imaginative temperament.[5] The Preface shows that this scepticism is not only turned in, as it were, to his fictional world, but outwards to his

[5] *Literary Studies* (2 vols., London: Dent, 1911) II, p. 128.

reader as well. Part of the purpose of the 'Novel without a Hero' is to probe and question the habitual assumptions the reader brings with him to reading a novel, sometimes to the extent of deliberately discomposing his normal confidence in the author. This means that the narrator of *Vanity Fair* is a much less stable and consistent presence than the narrator of *Tom Jones*, say, or *Middlemarch*, where we seem to feel the authority of the writer's own voice in the narration. Thackeray's narrator is more dramatically conceived and helps to make the commentary itself dramatic, and the reader in his turn needs to be alert to the narrator's changing tones and attitudes and not be too quick to identify them with Thackeray himself.

There is a final point about the Preface which is worth bearing in mind. It is such an assured piece of writing, fits so beautifully with the last sentence of the novel, that it is tempting to take the melancholy, detached Manager of the puppet-show as the controlling image of the narrator in *Vanity Fair*. But not only did Thackeray write the Preface after he had completed the novel, he did not introduce the notion of puppetry into the text or illustrations until the end either. As Joan Stevens points out,[6] in the earlier chapters 'Thackeray's recurrent image is that of the clown-moralist' addressing a congregation of 'brother wearers of motley' (ch. 19). The detached perspective is appropriate for the beginning and the end, but the narrator we meet in the body of the novel is a much more involved, and compromised, figure.

[6] 'A Note on Thackeray's "Manager of the Performance"', *Nineteenth Century Fiction* XXII (1967–8), pp. 391–7.

1. Beginning the World

(Monthly numbers I–V, chapters 1–18)

Vanity Fair opens with a memorable act of defiance, as Becky throws her copy of the Dictionary back into Miss Pinkerton's garden. The fact that it should be Dr Johnson's Dictionary adds a certain period piquancy to the scene. If Becky at this moment is youth rejecting age, she is also the rebellious spirit of the new nineteenth century rejecting the dying remnants of the eighteenth, for the time of the action ('While the present century was in its teens') has been carefully placed in the period of the Napoleonic Wars and the years immediately before Waterloo in 1815. Thackeray uses Miss Pinkerton's cult of the 'Great Lexicographer' to underline her snobbish and parasitic relationship to eighteenth-century decorum, and also to reveal, through the empty periphrastic style of her letters, how lifeless the old forms have become. Johnson's Christian stoicism and complex commitment to reason and order have dwindled to the stiffening proprieties of the finishing-school ('a careful and undeviating use of the backboard,' she writes to Amelia's parents, 'for four hours daily during the next three years, is recommended as necessary to the achievement of that dignified *deportment and carriage*, so requisite for every young lady of *fashion*'). It is fitting that the challenge to the 'stately old brick house' in Chiswick Mall should come from Becky, who with her command of French and admiration for Napoleon is aware of a larger world beyond the insular gentility of Miss Pinkerton's Academy.

> 'But that talking French to Miss Pinkerton was capital fun, wasn't it? She doesn't know a word of French, and was too proud to confess it. I believe it was that which made her part with me; and so thank Heaven for French. *Vive la France! Vive l'Empereur! Vive Bonaparte!*'
>
> (ch. 2)

Becky's knowledge of French is a source of comic power in the novel; it marks her difference from cosseted English girls like Amelia, and later from the ladies of fashion, who speak it less well than she does. Further, it links her in an ironic parallel with Napoleon which Thackeray exploits both for satirical purposes – like Napoleon, Becky is an upstart challenging the old order – and for narrative cohesion, as one of the many threads binding the ordinary lives of the characters to the larger world of history.

That opening gesture tells us a good deal about Becky, about her spirit, her independence, her capacity for cruelty. The sight of the Dictionary coming back over the wall is irresistibly comic and stirring, a justified response to all the condescension she has received at Chiswick, until one remembers that the giver is not Miss Pinkerton but her tender-hearted sister Jemima, and that it has been offered in a spirit of kindness and sympathy (the callous streak which this action reveals is further emphasized in Thackeray's illustration, where the expression on Becky's face is hard and malicious). The mixture of sympathy and recoil evoked by this scene is to constitute the pattern of our experience of Becky in the novel; we register the justice in her defiance of an unjust society but are repelled by her treachery and hardness of heart. The distancing effect is deliberate: Thackeray does not want us to identify with Becky as we may do, say, with a comparable figure like the heroine of Charlotte Brontë's contemporaneous *Jane Eyre* (1847). Becky is not, like Jane, a moral heroine engaged in an emotional and spiritual pilgrimage, although there are some superficial resemblances between their stories – both are orphans, for example, who have to struggle against the condescension or indifference of respectable society, both become governesses, both novels open with acts of rebellion. But whereas *Jane Eyre* invites the sympathetic involvement of the reader, Thackeray's irony keeps it at bay.

The source of this irony, at least in the early chapters, is the discrepancy between the novelistic convention of the *ingénue*, the young inexperienced heroine adrift in the world, and the reality of Becky's thorough worldliness. 'The History of a Young Lady's Entrance into the World' is the subtitle of Fanny Burney's popular epistolary novel *Evelina* (1778), a very influential sentimental-cum-fashionable work which Thackeray parodies in chapter 8 when Becky writes to Amelia of her experiences with the Crawley family. Evelina is an orphan, described in the novel's Preface as 'a young woman of obscure birth, but conspicuous beauty', who has been 'educated in the most secluded retirement' and 'makes, at the age of seventeen, her first appearance upon the great and busy stage of life; with a virtuous mind, a cultivated understanding, and a feeling heart'. These words might conceivably describe Amelia, who is 17 when the novel opens, but they are comically inappropriate to Becky, who has made her 'Entrance into the World' much earlier, in the debt and bohe-mianism of her artist father's home. There she has acquired, with 'the dismal precocity of poverty' (ch. 2), some unconventional skills to com-pensate for the early loss of innocence, skills of mimicry and dissimulation as well as — a rare endowment this in the heroine of an early Victorian novel — ease in and enjoyment of the company of men. Much of the fun at the start comes from the spectacle of Becky acting out what had become by Thackeray's time a narrative cliché, as she plays the unpro-tected orphan in the Sedley family and sings sentimental songs, while secretly angling for the bashful, wealthy Jos.

If Becky is a false *ingénue*, Amelia is a real one, although no more immune from Thackeray's irony for being so. Both heroines involve pit-falls for the unwary reader: in Becky's case to see her only as a spirited rebel, in Amelia's to dismiss or sentimentalize her as a conventional heroine. In fact Thackeray is probing and testing cliché here too, the cliché of 'the kind, fresh, smiling, artless, tender little domestic goddess, whom men are inclined to worship' (ch. 12). Amelia is introduced in terms that tease us with conventional images of feminine virtue and accomplishment; she deserves all Miss Pinkerton's praises, the narrator affirms, her classmates love her, she sings like a lark and embroiders beautifully:

> But as we are to see a great deal of Amelia, there is no harm in saying, at the outset of our acquaintance, that she was a dear little creature; and a great mercy it is, both in life and in novels, which (and the latter especially) abound in villains of the most sombre sort, that we are to have for a constant companion, so guileless and good-natured a person.
>
> (ch. 1)

The terms of praise here are slightly condescending ('dear little creature', 'guileless and good-natured') and the irony, playing between 'life' and 'novels', implicitly questions the ideas of life we take from fiction. When Thackeray then goes on to observe that 'her nose was rather short than otherwise, and her cheeks a great deal too round and red for a heroine', fundamental doubts have been insinuated. The course of the novel will test this model pupil and all model notions of heroism, asking how well the conventional qualities stand up to the experience of life, unearthing a mixed human reality beneath the domestic ideal.

By distancing us from both Becky and Amelia, Thackeray's irony invites the reader to find his interest not in identification with the destiny of a single protagonist but in the parallels and contrasts between two characters whose natures seem morally opposed but whose stories converge at many points. We start with an antithesis that has all the stark simplicity of Romance (although Thackeray reverses the usual formula by making his 'bad' heroine fair and his 'good' heroine dark): Becky is active where Amelia is passive, knowing where she is naïve, witty and articulate where she relies on dumb feeling. The difference between them could even be described in some such large general terms as an opposition between worldliness and unworldliness. But as the novel develops and their stories run parallel – both leaving school together, seeking husbands, marrying soldiers, going to Brussels and Waterloo – the reader becomes involved in a continual process of comparison which starts to loosen the hard edge of the initial antithesis. Unconventional insights emerge: we quickly realize that Becky's irreverence has a certain moral validity as a response to the snobbish, money-worshipping society portrayed in *Vanity Fair*, and that her worldly acumen is a source of laughter and satire. Amelia's maidenly devotion to George suddenly looks blind and foolish when we see him through Becky's sharp eyes, admiring himself in the mirror in chapter 5, and Becky's spirited and realistic response to limited opportunities makes us aware that Amelia's unworldliness is not as straightforward as it seemed at first, that it is made possible by the cushion of wealth and conceals selfishness and sentimentality too. In other words, any disposition the reader may have had to see the characters in simple moral categories is soon being tested.

The running parallel and contrast between Amelia and Becky provides the narrative backbone of *Vanity Fair*, but the same principle of pairing and contrast between characters is at work elsewhere, amplifying and enriching the baldness of the original opposition between worldliness and unworldliness, and adding further dimensions to the theme of vanity in the novel.[1] Thus the introduction of Dobbin, another unworldly character, at the start of the second monthly number (chs. 5–7), helps to bring into focus the question of *style* as a manifestation of vanity. His very name suggests plodding clumsiness, and with his lisp and unfashionable

---

[1] See here Myron Taube, 'Contrast as a Principle of Structure in *Vanity Fair*', *Nineteenth Century Fiction* XVIII (1963–4), pp. 119–35; and Peter K. Garrett, *The Victorian Multiplot Novel* (New Haven: Yale University Press, 1980), pp. 95–134.

appearance he makes an immediate contrast to his dandy friends, George Osborne and Jos Sedley. A more subtle pairing, however, the kind of structural detail only noticed on rereading a novel, is the one that links Dobbin and Becky. There is a hint of it in the suggested parallel between the opening chapters of the first and second numbers, where Dobbin's fight with Cuff at Dr Swishtail's Academy in chapter 5 recalls Becky's much more elegant and assured defiance of Miss Pinkerton in the first scene.[2] In the short run Dobbin's plain, unfashionable decency highlights both the comic narcissism of the overdressed Jos and the more insidious narcissism of the pseudo-Byronic George (as, for example, when George buys a diamond shirt-pin for himself with the money Dobbin gives him to buy a present for Amelia). But in the longer run the pairing in contrast of Dobbin and Becky counts for more: the man without style and the woman who can mimic all styles are in their different ways the principal agents in Thackeray's exposure of the vanity of style in the world of the novel.

Dobbin remains a relatively undeveloped character in the early chapters, however, and it is Becky who takes the eye. From the moment of rejecting the Dictionary to the cliff-hanging close of IV (ch. 14), where Sir Pitt proposes and Becky announces that she is already married, her rapid social progress contrasts with the static solitude of Amelia, waiting with mounting desperation for the proposal from George that comes at the end of V (ch. 18). Amelia's conventional passivity, 'absorbed still in one selfish, tender thought, and quite regardless of all the world besides' (ch. 18), throws Becky's energy and resourcefulness into a favourable light. It is hard not to admire her resilience as she copes with Jos's drunkenness at Vauxhall and the expected proposal that never comes, or her response to the dismal Crawley town house where she has to share her bed with the charwoman: 'Rebecca sprang about the apartment . . . with the greatest liveliness, and had peeped into the huge wardrobes, and the closets, and the cupboards, and tried the drawers which were locked, and examined the dreary pictures and toilette appointments, while the old charwoman was saying her prayers' (ch. 7). Her restless curiosity is a principle of life and energy in the novel, lighting up her dreary surroundings in this scene and later the dullness and

[2] See the discussion of this and other structural parallels in Edgar F. Harden, 'The Discipline and Significance of Form in *Vanity Fair*', *PMLA* LXXXII (1967), pp. 530–41.

stupidity of many of the characters she meets in her upward progress.

We may also be disposed to sympathize with Becky out of an awareness of the forces of money and respectability ranged against her. As
Barbara Hardy has shown,[3] Thackeray is very good at suggesting the
imposing solidity of wealth in his society, the way the rich at a time of
rapid commercial expansion tended to display their money in heavy
material terms: fat servants, rich clothes, heavy furniture, large meals all
figure prominently in his novels. Objects and possessions dominate the
lives and emotions of many of his characters, such as George Osborne's
sister Maria:

> Miss Maria Osborne, it is true, was 'attached' to Mr Frederic
> Augustus Bullock, of the firm of Hulker, Bullock & Bullock; but hers
> was a most respectable attachment, and she would have taken Bullock
> Senior, just the same, her mind being fixed as that of a well-bred
> young woman should be, – upon a house in Park Lane, a country
> house at Wimbledon, a handsome chariot, and two prodigious tall
> horses and footmen, and a fourth of the annual profits of the eminent
> firm of Hulker & Bullock, all of which advantages were represented in
> the person of Frederic Augustus.
>
> (ch. 12)

(One notes in passing the brilliance of Thackeray's names, 'Hulker &
Bullock' catching just the right degree of heavy, stupid materiality.) In
this world of domineering possessions there is considerable satirical point
in the fact that Becky starts out poor and undersized, looking 'like a
child' beside the 'many tall and bouncing young ladies in [Miss Pinkerton's] establishment' (ch. 2). Our knowledge of her early deprivation
brings home the cushioning power of wealth in this society, from the 'fat
coachman' and the 'two fat horses' in the first paragraph to fat, gorman-
dizing Jos Sedley himself. It also makes her social ambition more difficult
to judge unequivocally: in a world where condescension and insult are the
lot of the genteel poor like Miss Briggs, where even Mr Sedley's groom
can mock her when out of his employer's earshot (' "I hope you've
forgot nothink? Miss 'Melia's gownds – have you got them – as the
lady's-maid was to have 'ad? I hope they'll fit you." ' [ch. 7]), Becky's
determination to climb into a sphere where her considerable talents will

[3] *The Exposure of Luxury: Radical Themes in Thackeray* (London: Peter Owen,
1972), pp. 95–117.

be recognized is all too understandable – and on the worst construction no more ignoble than the determination of the respectable Maria Osborne to live off the profits of Hulker & Bullock.

There is a further dimension to our experience of Becky in these early chapters which may incline us towards her, despite her faults, and that is a kind of implicit, possibly unconscious alliance between her skills as a mimic and actress and Thackeray's own skills as a satirical novelist of manners. 'I like Becky in that book', he is reported as saying later in life. 'Sometimes I think I have myself some of her tastes.'[4] Certainly Becky is endowed with some of her creator's talents. She is, for example, a considerable narrative artist in her own right, continually inventing and re-inventing the story of her life. She is never at a loss for an explanation in a crisis, even when taken by surprise, as she is by Lord Steyne when he discovers what she has done with the money to pay Miss Briggs: 'Becky was only a little taken aback. . . . and in an instant she was ready with another neat, plausible, circumstantial story which she administered to her patron' (ch. 52). Like Thackeray again, Becky is a brilliant parodist, and her mimicry of various stereotyped social roles is the instrument of his parody. She performs the helpless *ingénue* in the Sedley home, the sentimental friend when writing to Amelia, a 'serious' (i.e. Evangelical) young woman of reforming sympathies when talking to Mr Crawley: 'She admired, beyond measure, his speech at the Quashimaboo-Aid Society; took an interest in his pamphlet on malt; was often affected, even to tears, by his discourses of an evening, and would say – "Oh, thank you, sir," with a sigh, and a look up to heaven' (ch. 10). By mimicking conventional behaviour Becky makes it comic, and Thackeray's narrative tone tends to comply with her exploits; as the agent of his satirical exposure she is the beneficiary of his and our enjoyment of the satire.

Becky's subversive mimicry of the conventional makes her a peculiarly appropriate central character for a novel which itself gets under way by mimicry, by mocking and subverting the tones and conventions of contemporary fiction. Thackeray's long 10-year apprenticeship for *Vanity Fair* had been served as a writer of miscellaneous journalism – parodies, sketches, reviews, travel pieces, burlesques, satires – for *Fraser's Magazine* and later *Punch*, in its irreverent early Victorian phase. Even his attempts at longer fiction, such as *Catherine* (1839–40) and *The Luck of Barry Lyndon* (1844), had been largely parodic in conception, reflecting his critical hostility to the popular fiction of the day. There is a considerable carry-over from these activities in the first two monthly numbers (chs. 1–7) of *Vanity Fair*, much of which may in any case have been written separately and earlier than the rest of the novel.[5] 'We might have treated this subject in the genteel, or in the romantic, or in the facetious manner', the narrator muses in chapter 6, and then takes the reader behind the scenes to sketch out 'supremely genteel', 'entirely low' and violently melodramatic versions of his story (these were much more fully developed in the first edition). 'But my readers must hope for no such romance, only a homely story, and must be content with a chapter about Vauxhall, which is so short that it scarce deserves to be called a chapter at all.' The narrative voice is initially sceptical of the grander claims of fiction as an art. Seemingly insignificant objects are lifted into ironic prominence (a green silk purse, a glass of punch), and the novelist's power to create glamour and suspense is mocked by Thackeray's frequent apologies for the mildness of his tale and the humdrum people with which it deals.

These acts of narrative refusal may be partly a legacy from his *Punch* writings, but they serve a more serious purpose as well. By reminding us of the necessary gap between the illusions about life encouraged by sensational or romantic novels and the reality, Thackeray is clearing the ground for that steady contemplation of ordinary undramatic life which is what his contemporaries saw as his pioneering realism:

> I know that the tune I am piping is a very mild one, (although there are some terrific chapters coming presently,) and must beg the good-natured reader to remember, that we are only discoursing at present about a stock-broker's family in Russell Square, who are taking walks, or luncheon, or dinner, or talking and making love as people do in common life, and without a single passionate and wonderful incident to mark the progress of their loves.
>
> (ch. 6)

Thackeray's defence of 'common life' as a fictional subject was both a blow for realism and an assertion of the validity of a middle-class or

[5] For a discussion of the complicated (and still disputed) planning of the novel, see the Introduction by Geoffrey and Kathleen Tillotson to the Methuen/Riverside edition of *Vanity Fair*, pp. xvii–xx.

bourgeois scope for the novel. The falsifying fictions he is attacking in *Vanity Fair* are the so-called 'silver fork' or fashionable novels of Mrs Gore and Disraeli, and the novels of military adventure, often with a Napoleonic setting, of Charles Lever and others. No one reads Mrs Gore or Charles Lever today, but one can catch their flavour and get a sense of what Thackeray was attacking by reading his parodies of them in *Novels by Eminent Hands* (sometimes called *Punch's Prize Novelists*) in any collected edition of his works. In 'Lords and Liveries' Thackeray brilliantly mocks Mrs Gore's novels of high society, alternately snobbish and sentimental, and written in a gushing style spattered with Gallicisms. Thackeray's spoof of Lever — 'Phil Fogarty. A Tale of the Fighting Onety-Oneth. By Harry Rollicker' — parodies just those features of military fiction his own novel was to eschew — rollicking accounts of battle with the reality of bloodshed and death obscured, and ludicrous historical name-dropping ('I and Prince Talleyrand danced a double hornpipe with Pauline Bonaparte and Madame de Stael'). In *Vanity Fair* he makes fun of the military campaign by transposing it into a domestic setting and exploiting its mock-heroic possibilities, especially in his chapter titles: 'In which Miss Sharp and Miss Sedley prepare to open the Campaign' (ch. 2), 'Rebecca is in Presence of the Enemy' (ch. 3), 'In which Amelia invades the Low Countries' (ch. 28). Conversely, he elevates domestic over military realities by making them the focus of his attention in the Waterloo section. The result is not just a simple debunking of the heroic but an immensely more powerful and sympathetic account of war's impact on the lives of ordinary men and women. Thackeray's narrative refusals pay rich dividends: by keeping Napoleon in the wings as an 'august mute personage' (ch. 18), by concentrating on the sufferings of the non-combatants and on the aftermath of war, the awesome reality of Waterloo is brought home in a way that it never is in the military novels.

'Coming as it did into the world of fiction occupied by the writers burlesqued in the *Novels by Eminent Hands*,' the Victorian critic W. C. Brownell observed of *Vanity Fair*, 'its substitution of truth for convention had something almost fierce in it.'[6] If the first two monthly numbers are playful and irreverent in their handling of convention, ferocity makes itself felt in the third (chs. 8–11). Thackeray's target here is the snobbish

---

[6] W. C. Brownell, *Victorian Prose Masters* (1902), p. 33; quoted by Kathleen Tillotson, *Novels of the Eighteen-Forties* (Oxford: Clarendon Press, 1954), p. 228.

and romantic impression of genteel life conveyed by the novels of fashion. 'Sir Pitt is not what we silly girls, when we used to read *Cecilia* at Chiswick, imagined a baronet must have been', Becky writes to Amelia. 'Anything, indeed, less like Lord Orville cannot be imagined' (ch. 8). Thackeray has got his Burney novels mixed up: Lord Orville is the model aristocrat of *Evelina*, not *Cecilia*, and it is the epistolary technique of the former – and of course of Samuel Richardson's novel in letters, *Sir Charles Grandison* (1753–4), the ultimate source of the sentimental–fashionable school – that is being parodied here and in the three letters in chapter 11. These are the period equivalents, in the second decade of the century when the novel is set, of the fashionable novels with which Thackeray's mid-century readers were familiar. The attack is indeed fierce: 'Fancy an old, stumpy, short, vulgar, and very dirty man, in old clothes and shabby old gaiters, who smokes a horrid pipe, and cooks his own horrid supper in a saucepan. He speaks with a country accent, and swore a great deal at the old charwoman'. Nothing could be more remote from fictional paragons like Lord Orville and Sir Charles Grandison, and the attack on false notions of genteel society continues in the portrait of life at Queen's Crawley in chapters 9 and 10, and in the broad irony of chapter 11, 'Arcadian Simplicity', which recounts the family rivalry for Miss Crawley's fortune. The mystique of gentry life is swept away as we see how greed and materialism have infected the squire and the parson:

> 'She drank cherry-brandy after dinner,' continued his Reverence, 'and took curaçao with her coffee. *I* wouldn't take a glass for a five-pound note: it kills me with heart-burn. She can't stand it, Mrs Crawley – she must go – flesh and blood won't bear it! and I lay five to two, Matilda drops in a year.'

But the reader is not allowed to laugh at the Reverend Bute and Sir Pitt with too comfortable a detachment, either. He has already been reminded in chapter 9 of the great difference 'that balance at the banker's' makes to his own treatment of his wealthy maiden aunt: 'What a good fire there is in her room when she comes to pay you a visit, although your wife laces her stays without one! . . . Is it so, or is it not so? I appeal to the middle classes.' The middle classes are kept on the hop too by the uncomfortable voice of the narrator, which has by now found its true range after some earlier uncertainty; its shifting, probing irony continually mediates between the characters and the world of the reader, implicating him in the critique of vanity and depriving him of the consolations of moral detachment. This alternation and interaction between narrative and commentary is the heartbeat of *Vanity Fair*, and it is starting to pulse strongly.

In discussing the novel so far I have paid some attention to the disposition of the chapters within the monthly number divisions, and these will repay scrutiny by anyone studying the structure of *Vanity Fair*. A Victorian serial novelist in full flood had to give a little of everything in each monthly number, if possible, and to preserve design in the part as well as the whole, if he was to keep the interest of his readers from month to month. Ideally, each number needed to be a microcosm of the whole and at the same time convey an impression of forward movement and unfolding action. These often taxing requirements encouraged devices of analogy, parallelism and contrast as means of orchestrating a large cast of characters and keeping sub-plots in motion and interaction with the main plot. Thackeray eschews sub-plot but makes extensive use of parallelism and contrast, as we have seen, both within the monthly number and between numbers. The transition from III to IV (chs. 12–14) is a good example of these devices at work, enriched by the additional effect produced by a tonal shift from 'satire' to 'sentiment'. At a fairly obvious level, there is the contrast between the active and aspiring Becky, who dominates III and whose fortunes are moving upwards in the Crawley family, and Amelia, passive and becalmed, whose fortunes in IV are starting to tip downwards. There are the parallels between two fathers and two sons, Sir Pitt Crawley in Hampshire and Mr Osborne in Russell Square, both boorish and bullying, and Rawdon Crawley and George Osborne, both officers (though Rawdon in a far smarter regiment), both selfish, one falling in love with a woman who has too little affection to offer him in return, the other beloved by a woman who has if anything too much. And there is the contrast of tone, the hard-edged satire of the Queen's Crawley chapters being followed by two avowedly 'sentimental' chapters dealing with Amelia.

The question of tone here is tricky. The very chapter-headings put us on our guard and the treatment of Amelia is hedged by irony. The narrator envisages a female correspondent who finds her '*fade* and insipid' and then retorts weakly that men, after all, prefer her type. But the irony with which she is presented seems to concede the criticism:

Poor little tender heart! and so it goes on hoping and beating, and longing and trusting. You see it is not much of a life to describe.

There is not much of what you call incident in it. Only one feeling all
day – when will he come? only one thought to sleep and wake
upon.

(ch. 12)

It is difficult to know what weight to give to 'tender' here. The narrator
tends to see as the world sees, and the irony tells against the worldly
reader who can find no interest in this unworldly life. But 'only one feeling' and 'only one thought' suggests there is also an uncomfortable criticism of Amelia at work here, that her obsession with George is stupid and
selfish ('The fate of Europe was Lieutenant George Osborne to her'). The
ambivalence of tone may well reflect an ambivalence in Thackeray himself, and not just in his narrator. The impression left by these chapters is
of 'sentiment' qualified by irony, but not ironized away, and so continu-
ing to exist as a moral and tonal resource in the novel to be drawn upon to
greater effect later.

A bolder use of 'sentiment' can be seen, for example, in chapter 17 of
the next monthly number (V: chs. 15–18), which describes the auction
at the Sedley home. 'If there is any exhibition in all Vanity Fair which
Satire and Sentiment can visit arm in arm together; where you light on
the strangest contrasts laughable and tearful: where you may be gentle
and pathetic, or savage and cynical with perfect propriety: it is at one of
those public assemblies'. It is characteristic of Thackeray that the
moment in the novel when 'Satire and Sentiment' are brought into effective partnership, and those 'contrasts' of irony and feeling balanced,
should be in the description of an auction, for auctions are invariably
suggestive spectacles in his work. An auction is a social occasion in which
Vanity Fair comes to contemplate the instability of life in Vanity Fair,
bringing back memories of the time when the lights shone in the
evening, there was food and drink on the table and witty company to be
had. It prompts reflections on the ironies of fortune, which have brought
a greedy and vulgar crowd of auctioneers and agents to prey on the ship-
wreck of the prosperous ('O Dives, who would ever have thought, as we
sat round the broad table sparkling with plate and spotless linen, to have
seen such a dish at the head of it as that roaring auctioneer?'). And it
offers the poignant spectacle of privacy invaded, of indifferent fingers
'poking into the feathers, shampooing the mattresses, and clapping the
wardrobe drawers to and fro'. Even Becky is 'entirely surprised at the
sight of the comfortable old house where she had met with no small kindness, ransacked by brokers and bargainers, and its quiet family treasures

given up to public desecration and plunder'. In all these respects the auction engages most of Thackeray's central concerns in the novel; it is like the Fair described in the Preface, a 'bustling place' which gives rise in the observer to 'a feeling of profound melancholy'.

The Sedley auction is the pivotal scene in the fifth monthly number, and one might note the skilful way in which it not only combines 'Satire and Sentiment' in itself, but effects a bridge between these different tones in the two halves of the number. As an event in the 'world' it is an appropriate place for the newly married Becky and Rawdon to go, fresh and lively with schemes to part Miss Crawley and her money (chs. 15 and 16); but as a witness to the Sedley defeat it leads us back into Amelia's world of private suffering. Again, the contrast between the two heroines is unobtrusively effective. The number begins with Sir Pitt at the married Becky's feet; it ends with George Osborne's last-ditch proposal to Amelia, which he has been prodded into making by Dobbin; begins with satire, in other words, and ends with sentiment. It also adds a new dimension to our understanding of Becky and Amelia in terms of their attitude to time. Becky quickly overcomes her regrets for having missed Sir Pitt, for she 'was a young lady of too much resolution and energy of character to permit herself much useless and unseemly sorrow for the irrevocable past' (ch. 15). Amelia comes to live more and more in the past, as she broods over George's 'worthless' letters: 'She lived in her past life — every letter seemed to recal [sic] some circumstance of it' (ch. 18) — a tendency which marriage will scarcely interrupt. These contrasts are made more dramatic and suggestive by the fact that Thackeray chooses to interrupt chronology and place the public event of the auction *before* the explanation of the bankruptcy and the causes that led up to it. Since the chief of these causes is the return of Napoleon to France, the effect is to bring the larger world of 'history' into the forefront just when the narrative focus is on the 'private' world of Amelia's suffering:

> So imprisoned and tortured was this gentle little heart, when in the month of March, Anno Domini 1815, Napoleon landed at Cannes, and Louis XVIII fled, and all Europe was in alarm, and the funds fell, and old John Sedley was ruined.
>
> (ch. 18)

This conjunction of the resurgent Napoleon and the 'gentle little heart' is so of the essence of Thackeray's vision of history that it leads inevitably to the question of *Vanity Fair* as a historical novel, which my next chapter must take up.

2. Fashion and War

(Monthly numbers VI–IX, chapters 19–32)

The next four numbers move with increasing momentum to the battle of Waterloo which, taking place offstage, is Thackeray's most brilliant and important narrative refusal in *Vanity Fair*. Although the battle itself is given only a short paragraph in the text, its presence seems to bulk large in our experience of the novel. Waterloo is a decisive event in the lives of the principal characters and in the life of their society; it is an historical event, serving, as Avrom Fleishman says, to 'fix events in historical time more firmly than in any other novel of the age';[1] it is a touchstone of reality, throwing its great shadow of loss and pain across the lives of the characters and showing up the shallowness and triviality of most of their concerns. Above all, in Thackeray's handling Waterloo is an event within Vanity Fair itself, for he continually emphasizes the concurrence of the military and the fashionable campaigns by bringing Becky to the 'perpetual military festival' at Brussels, 'where all the Vanity Fair booths were laid out with the most tempting liveliness and splendour' (ch. 28), and making it the scene of her social triumph. It is this interplay between fashion and war, coming to a splendid climax in the escape from Brussels of the fat dandy Jos Sedley, which keeps Waterloo within the comic, satiric mode of the novel while allowing its more serious implications to emerge through force of contrast.

Waterloo was fought in 1815; *Vanity Fair* started to appear in 1847: to what extent should it be considered an historical novel? This is not an easy question to answer decisively. Like many other famous Victorian novels, as Kathleen Tillotson has demonstrated,[2] *Vanity Fair* falls into that curious middle distance of time, the day before yesterday, distinct from the contemporary scene but not quite remote enough to seem historical in the accepted sense. George Eliot is a comparable case: with the exception of *Daniel Deronda*, all her novels of English life are set back in time some 30 to 60 years from the date of their writing and publication

---

[1] *The English Historical Novel* (Baltimore: Johns Hopkins Press, 1971), p. 146.
[2] *Novels of the Eighteen-Forties*, pp. 91–115.

– *Middlemarch* from 1871- 2 to the time of the First Reform Bill in 1832. Again, *Wuthering Heights* was published in 1847, but opens in 1801, and its action reaches back into the second half of the eighteenth century. But these and other novels are domestic and regional in scope, with at most a glancing relation to public events. Waterloo is a great historical landmark, and its central position in the structure of *Vanity Fair* must make for a certain difference. Perhaps the nearest parallel is not with an English novel at all, or with the historical romances of Walter Scott, but with Tolstoy's *War and Peace*, published 20 years later than Thackeray's novel in 1868–9, but also looking back to the Napoleonic Wars at the start of the century. As in *War and Peace*, the historical dimension is important but not ultimately distinct from contemporary life or general human experience, unlike the historical novel proper, which offers the distinctness, the otherness of the past as its chief source of interest. *Vanity Fair* can be read, I would suggest, on three temporal levels:

1. As a timeless and universally applicable statement about the power of selfishness and pride in human affairs, and a vision of the vanity of earthly things as old as Ecclesiastes ('Vanity of vanities, saith the Preacher, vanity of vanities: all is vanity').

2. As a novel of 1846, satirizing the snobbery and social climbing of a time when the influx of new wealth from industrialization and the rise of stockjobbing was loosening the old class barriers and providing opportunities for parvenus like Becky. On this level *Vanity Fair* is best read in conjunction with Thackeray's *Book of Snobs*, published almost concurrently in *Punch* as *The Snobs of England*.

3. As a novel of 1815 and its aftermath.

These three levels are held together naturally by the narrator, whose memory encompasses the novel's entire historical range, and no more than in *War and Peace* is one obliged to choose between them.

Nonetheless, it is worth thinking about the novel of 1815, particularly in relation to what Tolstoy does with a very similar stretch of history in *War and Peace*. As John Carey says, *Vanity Fair* 'is the only English novel of . . . [the Victorian] period which, in theme and range, challenges comparison with *War and Peace*'.[3] It is a bold claim, one that even Thackeray's admirers have been slow to make, and yet, I believe, essentially just. In the first place, *Vanity Fair* is almost unique among Victorian

[3] *Thackeray: Prodigal Genius* (London: Faber, 1977), p. 177.

novels in giving us the Tolstoyan sense of the individual life enmeshed in the great events of history. This may seem an extravagant statement, given the acknowledged density of social registration in Victorian fiction and the irony with which Thackeray handles the subject. But the sense of history in the great Victorian novels is almost invariably domestic, local, urban or regional in character; they have a great deal to say about social change, but war and its upheavals pass them by, no doubt because such experiences passed the society by as well. Thackeray knew, however, that the Victorian peace had been made possible by a great battle, that Waterloo had been formative in shaping the direction and character of nineteenth-century society, and his novel is partly a meditation on that fact. Of course his treatment of war is oblique and mainly comic; there is nothing in *Vanity Fair* to compare with Tolstoy' extensive treatment of the battles of Austerlitz and Borodino, the retreat from Moscow, the deaths of Prince Andrew and Pétya Rostóv. By contrast, the death of George Osborne takes only three lines, albeit three lines of explosive force. Yet Thackeray's obliqueness serves a similar purpose, one could argue. From the early comic hints – Becky's '*Vive Bonaparte!*' in chapter 2, Mrs Salmon's 'savage Cantata against the Corsican upstart' at Vauxhall (ch. 6) – to the falling of the funds, the bankrupting of John Sedley, Mr Osborne's opposition to Amelia, on to the marriage and George's death at Waterloo, there is a steadily mounting pressure on the characters from seemingly remote events, a sense of the individual caught in the grip of vast impersonal forces.

> *Bon Dieu*, I say, is it not hard that the fateful rush of the great Imperial struggle can't take place without affecting a poor little harmless girl of eighteen, who is occupied in billing and cooing, or working muslin collars in Russell Square? You, too, kindly, homely flower! – is the great roaring war tempest coming to sweep you down, here, although cowering under the shelter of Holborn? Yes; Napoleon is flinging his last stake, and poor little Emmy Sedley's happiness forms, somehow, part of it.
>
> (ch. 18)

One could go even further and speculate about the possible influence on *War and Peace* of *Vanity Fair*, which Tolstoy certainly admired and thought about. The idea of basing his novel around the destiny of three or four families may well have been suggested by Thackeray's broadly similar practice, and the anti-heroic emphasis of his commentary (although one senses it went against the grain of Tolstoy's own passionate individualism) is clearly derived from Thackeray. 'The ancients have left us model heroic poems in which the heroes furnish the whole interest of the story, and we are still unable to accustom ourselves to the fact that for our epoch histories of that kind are meaningless' − the words are Tolstoy's but their fictional implications had been worked out 20 years earlier in *Vanity Fair*.[4]

The really fruitful comparison for our purposes, though, concerns the setting of the two novels in the Napoleonic period. Tolstoy and Thackeray both saw the Napoleonic Wars as a turning-point in the historical development of their societies, but in rather different ways. For Tolstoy the battle of Borodino and Napoleon's retreat from Moscow marked a time of national resurgence. Just as Pierre Bezúkhov is reborn as a result of his experience as a prisoner-of-war with Napoleon's retreating armies, so in Tolstoy's view does Russia itself discover its true identity and the sources of its real strength. *War and Peace* becomes at the close a hymn to Russian nationhood. Thackeray, on the other hand, saw Waterloo as an end rather than a beginning, the last flourish of a military−aristocratic culture which valued public honour and heroism on the battlefield above the bourgeois code which had started to challenge it, the code of private conscience, domestic duty, respectability and earnestness. In its historical aspect, *Vanity Fair* is a meditation on the genesis of Victorianism, or in Gordon Ray's words, 'the capital illustration in literature of the revolution in manners that occurred between the reigns of George IV and Queen Victoria'.[5]

If the lord of *War and Peace* is space, as E. M. Forster remarked in *Aspects of the Novel*, then the lord of *Vanity Fair* is time. The effect of Waterloo and its aftermath is to sink the action deep in time and memory, to stimulate the narrator's own awareness of the past so that in turn we are made conscious of the memories of his characters, as they too look back on a receding landmark: these are to be major preoccupations

[4] Tolstoy, *War and Peace*, trans. Louise and Aylmer Maude (London: Macmillan and Oxford University Press, 1942), book X, ch. 19, p. 834.
[5] *Thackeray: the Uses of Adversity*, p. 418. For a full discussion of this topic, in relation to the changing conception of the 'gentleman', see R. Gilmour, *The Idea of the Gentleman in the Victorian Novel* (London: Allen & Unwin, 1981), pp. 37−71.

of the second half of the novel. Even the prospect of battle to come, which is increasingly emphasized in the section we are concerned with here, has a comparable effect of steadying and deepening the mood of the novel. Napoleon's return to France precipitates a crisis in the relations of Amelia and George, leading to their marriage and the disinheritance of George, and it also introduces an intermittent note of foreboding into the novel. Amelia's rainswept wedding, filtered to us through Dobbin's melancholy mood, seems to anticipate desolation: 'The rain came rattling down on the windows. In the intervals of the service you heard it, and the sobbing of old Mrs Sedley in the pew. The parson's tones echoed sadly through the empty walls' (ch. 22). And this chapter ends the sixth monthly number with the news that the regiment has been called to Belgium. As consequences become suddenly graver Thackeray shows several of the principal characters caught in moments of reflection, when the awakening of their memories adds almost a new dimension to our understanding of them. There is, for instance, Amelia's return to her family at Fulham and her awareness of the gulf that now separates her from her unmarried past:

She looked at the little white bed, which had been hers a few days before, and thought she would like to sleep in it that night, and wake, as formerly, with her mother smiling over her in the morning. Then she thought with terror of the great funereal damask pavilion in the vast and dingy state bed-room, which was awaiting her at the grand hotel in Cavendish Square. Dear little white bed! how many a long night had she wept on its pillow!

(ch. 26)

It is a superficial reading of *Vanity Fair* that sees this as an instance of Thackeray's sentimentality, or simply of Amelia's. She is sentimental, of course, but what is intimated here is her immaturity, her shocked discovery of how much she fears this long-desired marriage and the problems it has brought with it. Through the whole scene too runs the irony of disappointed expectations, linking it (but not at all reductively) to the theme of vanity: 'Already to be looking sadly and vaguely back: always to be pining for something which, when obtained, brought doubt and sadness rather than pleasure: here was the lot of our poor little creature, and harmless lost wanderer in the great struggling crowds of Vanity Fair.'

Another example of the new depth which enters the novel at this stage is the famous scene in which Mr Osborne scores his son's name out of the family Bible (ch. 24). It is too long to quote in full here, but the setting of the scene, as well as the act itself, is worth examining in detail. Thackeray begins by describing old Osborne's study in what are by now familiar satirical terms — the unread books in the glazed bookcases, the Bible and Prayer-Book standing 'beside his copy of the Peerage', the terror the place inspires in children and servants. 'George as a boy had been horse-whipped in this room many times; his mother sitting sick on the stair listening to the cuts of the whip.' The actuality of Osborne's brutal tyranny makes a mockery of the family picture over the mantelpiece, 'all with red cheeks and large red mouths, simpering on each other in the approved family-portrait manner', for the reality of this family is fear and estrangement. But as we see Osborne sitting alone in the dark, getting up to lock the door after his butler has brought the candles, and then settling to examine the son's letters he has so carefully kept, a new note enters the passage. It has to do — characteristically in Thackeray — with an awakening sense of the character's life in time, of the past that feeds the present. For in the carefully preserved and docketted letters, drawing-books, receipted bills and so on, we can see that Osborne has been a generous father to George ('Anything that money could buy had been his son's') and that his love for him is real too, although hopelessly contami-nated by selfishness and pride, and by the parvenu's hunger for vicarious social gratification ('Everybody said he was like a nobleman's son'). Thackeray gathers in this past and brings it to bear in a complex way on the sacrilegious act itself:

Then he opened the book-case, and took down the great red Bible we have spoken of — a pompous book, seldom looked at, and shining all over with gold. There was a frontispiece to the volume, representing Abraham sacrificing Isaac. Here according to custom, Osborne had recorded on the fly-leaf, and in his large clerk-like hand, the dates of his marriage and his wife's death, and the births and Christian names of his children. Jane came first, then George Sedley Osborne, then Maria Frances, and the days of the christening of each. Taking a pen, he carefully obliterated George's name from the page; and when the leaf was quite dry, restored the volume to the place from which he had moved it. Then he took a document out of another drawer, where his own private papers were kept; and having read it, crumpled it up and lighted it at one of the candles, and saw it burn entirely away in the grate. It was his will; which being burned, he sate down and wrote off a letter, and rang for his servant, whom he charged to deliver it in the morning. It was morning already: as he went up to bed: the whole house was alight with the sunshine; and the birds were singing among the fresh green leaves in Russell Square.

The only superfluous touch here is the overly allegorical reminder of Abraham and Isaac; everything else tells in a marvellously apt way. Osborne's 'large clerk-like hand' reminds us how he has risen from the ranks (by means of the Sedley whose godfatherhood is obliterated with George's name), as does the care with which he strikes out his son's name, waiting for the ink to dry before restoring the Bible, as if it were a ledger, to its proper place. The solemn precision with which the deed is done gives it the force of a terrible blasphemy – doubly so on a reread-ing, of course, when we know how close is George's death at Waterloo. And the house 'alight with the sunshine' in the last sentence, the birds 'singing among the fresh green leaves in Russell Square', rounds out the impurity of Osborne's action with a suggestion of the natural order against which it offends. All Thackeray's satirical concerns flow through this scene, but they are deepened, made at once more natural and more terrible, by the spectacle of the man's ignoble, baffled feelings for his son.

Such moments of reflection, when we catch the characters thinking about themselves and the past, make an effective contrast to the usual bustle of Vanity Fair preparing for war; Becky, one notes, is not given to introspection. They introduce a sympathetic element into the portrayal of characters we may have been inclined to dismiss rather too easily. This happens with George in a passage (ch. 29) which recalls the earlier scene with the family Bible. At the Waterloo Ball he flirts with Becky, drinks too much, starts to gamble, and then Dobbin comes with the news that the battle has started. At once he starts to think back over his life and feel remorse for the way he has treated Amelia and his father; and although this regret is 'selfish', the narrator says, it also serves to humanize him in our eyes:

Hope, remorse, ambition, tenderness, and selfish regret filled his heart. He sate down and wrote to his father, remembering what he had said once before, when he was engaged to fight a duel. Dawn faintly streaked the sky as he closed this farewell letter. He sealed it, and kissed the superscription. He thought how he had deserted that generous father, and of the thousand kindnesses which the stern old man had done him.

(ch. 29)

The 'farewell letter' and the dawn sky form a link with the earlier scene in Russell Square and make us aware of the unexpressed love between father and son, which will now never be expressed. It is this letter which is found in old Osborne's dressing-gown pocket at his death.

Chapter 29, and the eighth monthly number, end with the ensuing brief and touching scene of reconciliation between Amelia and George, but the account of the battle in IX (chs. 30–2) is in a rather different key. Having established a note of foreboding and deepened sympathy in these more quiet, reflective scenes, Thackeray reverts to a mainly comic treatment for the Waterloo number. There are serious notes here too, such as Dobbin catching sight of Amelia's face, 'so white, so wild and despair-stricken, that the remembrance of it haunted him afterwards like a crime' (ch. 30), but the prominence given to Becky and Jos ensures that the episode remains firmly within the comic and satirical frame. As the cannon of Waterloo boom in the background, we have the high comedy of Jos's rising panic, the shaving of his moustaches, and his ignominious flight from Brussels; and the spectacle of Becky, 'this dauntless world-ling' (ch. 31), at the height of her ambiguous powers – acting the part of the soldier's wife while secretly calculating her chances on Rawdon's death, fleecing Jos, making a fool of Lady Bareacres. A series of comic substitutions for the refused military action brings vanity and reality into satirical collision, a collision engineered largely in terms of the characters' attitudes to their possessions, particularly clothes and jewellery.

Thackeray was ambivalent about this, as about much less. He satirized luxury but his novels are full of exquisitely precise and sensuous descriptions of his characters' coats, dresses, rings, watches, canes, dressing-cases and other expensive items. These help to give his work its unique thickness of texture and to establish his own authority as an historian of manners.[6] But such items have an especially important place in *Vanity*

[6] This aspect of Thackeray's art has been brilliantly discussed by John Carey in his chapter on 'Commodities' in *Thackeray: Prodigal Genius*. See also Juliet McMaster's fine essay, 'Thackeray's Things: Time's Local Habitation', in Richard A. Levine, ed., *The Victorian Experience: The Novelists* (Ohio: Ohio University Press, 1976), pp. 49–86.

Fair, a novel much concerned with competing styles and the vanity of narcissism, and it is significant that they should figure prominently in the Waterloo chapters. On the one hand, Thackeray is interested in the sheer tenacity of the human urge to possess, even in the face of war and death – Becky taking stock of her trinkets while Rawdon marches off to battle, or Lady Bareacres sewing the family diamonds into her habit and her husband's padding and boots. His comic version of military spoil, the equivalent of the Homeric warrior stripping his victim's armour, is Isidor eyeing up his master's fashionable belongings as he dresses Jos:

> He would make a present of the silver essence-bottles and toilette knicknacks to a young lady of whom he was fond; and keep the English cutlery and the large ruby pin for himself. It would look very smart upon one of the fine frilled shirts, which, with the gold-laced cap and the frogged frock coat, that might easily be cut down to suit his shape, and the Captain's gold-headed cane, and the great double ring with the rubies, which he would have made into a pair of beautiful earrings, he calculated would make a perfect Adonis of himself, and render Mademoiselle Reine an easy prey. . . . So Jos's man was marking his victim down, as you see one of Mr. Paynter's assistants in Leadenhall-street ornament an unconscious turtle with a placard on which is written, 'Soup to-morrow.'
>
> (ch. 31)

The chances of war only sharpen the appetite for acquisition in Vanity Fair.

On the other hand, the ability to rise above the acquisitive urge, or make do with the worn and shabby rather than the brightly fashionable, becomes in these chapters an important indication of a character's worth. Amelia is indifferent to her appearance, but then her hysterical reaction to George's departure makes for a typically ambiguous comparison with Becky's almost heartless self-possession. A more telling contrast, again at the level of objects, is that between Peggy O'Dowd's big old watch, the 'repayther', which she uses to wake the Major after a night spent faithfully preparing his kit, and Becky's small fashionable ones ('a little bijou marked Leroy, with a chain and cover charmingly set with turquoises, and another signed Breguet, which was covered with pearls, and yet scarcely bigger than a half-crown'), adulterous gifts from George and General Tufto, which make her rooms 'alive with their clicking' (ch. 30). But the most surprising indifference to possessions, because it comes from a character we may have pigeon-holed as entirely worldly, is Rawdon's, when out of love for Becky he prepares a list of all his fashionable belongings – dressing-case, fur-lined cloak, 'chain and ticker', duelling-pistols ('same which I shot Captain Marker') – and leaves them behind for her to sell if need be, going off to battle 'in his oldest and shabbiest uniform and epaulets, leaving the newest behind, under his wife's (or it might be his widow's) guardianship. And this famous dandy of Windsor and Hyde Park went off on his campaign with a kit as modest as that of a serjeant, and with something like a prayer on his lips for the woman he was leaving' (ch. 30).

The renunciation of fashion which Rawdon makes willingly is forced on Jos Sedley by rumour and panic. Jos is the novel's chief narcissist, displaying in a gross but harmless and comic form the tendency to look in mirrors and adorn one's person which he shares with a more subtle narcissist like George Osborne. The 'stout civilian', as he is many times called, appears in Brussels dressed as a military dandy in his braided frock-coat, foraging cap and moustaches (one relishes the brilliance of Thackeray's comic substitution here, making Jos's experience of the war function in ironic counterpoint to that of the real soldiers offstage). Appropriately for this dandy narcissist, the moment of truth comes when at the height of his panic he catches sight of himself in the mirror:

Such is the force of habit, that even in the midst of his terror he began mechanically to twiddle with his hair, and arrange the cock of his hat. Then he looked amazed at the pale face in the glass before him, and especially at his mustachios, which had attained a rich growth in the course of near seven weeks, since they had come into the world. They *will* mistake me for a military man, thought he, remembering Isidor's warning, as to the massacre with which all the defeated British army was threatened; and staggering back to his bed-chamber, he began wildly pulling the bell which summoned his valet.

(ch. 32)

The interplay of fashion and war is brought to a splendid comic climax: the razor that shaves off the dandy's plumage stands in for the sabres that in a different kind of novel would be seen clashing at Quatre Bras. And the implications of this scene reach out beyond the comic subversion of military fiction to a larger symbolic meaning. Just as Jos loses his military-style frock-coat and expensive toilette items to Isidor, escaping from Brussels in a 'plain black coat' which makes him look like 'a flourishing, large parson of the Church of England', so too does the battle of Waterloo mark the beginning of the end of the quasi-aristocratic style of military dandyism as a dominant force in the world of the novel. One dandy has fled; another, George, is dead on the field; Rawdon has renounced his fashionable belongings. Dobbin survives, the plain, clumsy grocer's son who is utterly untouched by personal vanity, and he is to play an increasingly important part in the rest of the novel.

This, to return to my earlier comparison with *War and Peace*, is what I meant by saying that Thackeray saw Waterloo as an end rather than a beginning. The event marks the end of the characters' youth and, for all but Becky, of the flamboyance which goes with youth. What lies ahead for them is the slow accumulation of time and the testing of private experience. This sense of finality is rubbed home by the last paragraph of the Waterloo number:

> No more firing was heard at Brussels – the pursuit rolled miles away. Darkness came down on the field and city: and Amelia was praying for George, who was lying on his face, dead, with a bullet through his heart.
>
> (ch. 32)

One might note the precision of rhythm which, by isolating the word 'dead', accentuates its force, and also the religious pessimism implied in the parallel postures of the two characters – Amelia with her face in her hands praying, and George with his face on the earth, dead.

3. The Lengthening Perspective

(Monthly numbers X–XV, chapters 33–53)

In his study of Thackeray's methods of composition, *Thackeray at Work*, John Sutherland notes that whereas the first half of *Vanity Fair* is given to the two years before Waterloo, the second sprawls to take in the 25 years after it, and he observes: 'The large hazy expanses of the second half of the novel suit Thackeray's genius better than the clear but smaller scale of the first and it is characteristic of the novelist's empirical methods that this success should have been achieved not by more but by less strenuous time-keeping'.[1] It is a useful distinction and helps to explain a subtle but important development in Thackeray's narrative. The pre-Waterloo chapters are relatively compact and urgent because they lead up to the unavoidable historical event of the battle itself, but after Waterloo Thackeray can settle to a more leisurely pace and a much looser chronology. This seems to have suited Thackeray's genius better, as Dr Sutherland says, and to understand why this should have been so it is necessary to consider the significant part which retrospect plays in his mature narrative method.

The classic discussion of this aspect of Thackeray's art is in Percy Lubbock's *The Craft of Fiction* (1921), where Lubbock defines the novelist's 'peculiar mark, the distinction of his genius' as the tendency to hold everything in 'a long retrospective vision':

> He is a painter of life, a novelist whose matter is all blended and harmonized together – people, action, background – in a long retrospective vision. Not for him, on the whole, is the detached action, the rounded figure, the scenic rendering of a story; as surely as Dickens tended towards the theatre, with its clear-cut isolation of events and episodes, its underlining of the personal and the individual in men and women, so Thackeray preferred the manner of musing expatiation, where scene melts into scene, impressions are foreshortened by

[1] *Thackeray at Work*, p. 44.

distance, and the backward-ranging thought can linger and brood as it will.[2]

This well-known distinction between the 'scenic' or 'dramatic' method of Dickens, and Thackeray's 'panorama of manners' (p. 118), is helpful provided we do not make it too absolute. Obviously Thackeray uses something of both, and he is often at his most effective when he combines the leisurely panorama with the brilliantly lighted dramatic scene (as, supremely, in his account of Becky's downfall in XV, which I shall discuss later). But 'panorama' is sufficiently accurate to give us Thackeray's, or more precisely his narrator's, habitual stance before experience. He seems to stand apart from the action and to pick his story from an already existing world of people and events, and we seem to be aware of that world carrying on beyond the frame of the novel, of matter not included which might have been, or characters mentioned in passing as part of other histories the narrator lacks the time to tell. 'Thackeray's characters exist in a denser context than perhaps any characters in fiction', Kathleen Tillotson observes,[3] and she cites the case of the Edward Dale who buys the family's silver spoons at the Sedley auction and makes a present of them to Mrs Sedley.

> Edward Dale, the junior of the house, who purchased the spoons for the firm, was, in fact, very sweet upon Amelia, and offered for her in spite of all. He married Miss Louisa Cutts (daughter of Higham and Cutts, the eminent corn-factors), with a handsome fortune in 1820; and is now living in splendour, and with a numerous family, at his elegant villa, Muswell Hill.
>
> (ch. 17)

This is all we hear of him; another story surfaces briefly at the edge of our vision, complete with the authenticating details about Higham and Cutts and Muswell Hill, only to be crowded out by the pressure of other events. The impression is that of a world teeming with people and their stories, from which the narrator has been able to choose only a few.

The panoramic effect is temporal as well as spatial. The 'long retrospective vision' reaches back into the origins of Thackeray's society in the early years of the century, filling his canvas with details of the past

---

[2] *The Craft of Fiction* (London: Cape, 1921; 1965 edn.), p. 96.
[3] *Novels of the Eighteen-Forties*, p. 236.

– dates, songs, fashion, customs (like Vauxhall) – which cluster more thickly than in any other Victorian novelist and give an extra significance to his description of his novelist self as an 'historian'. The narrator's memory can command the genealogy of his high-born characters (such as the masterly description of the Steyne family in chapter 47) and the humble origins of his parvenus, and it seems to surround the characters, especially in the second half of *Vanity Fair*, with an awareness of their completed destinies, so that the 'story' often seems secondary to the reflections it occasions. The plot matters, needless to say: we want to know what happens next, but Thackeray's leisurely narrative method, interrupting chronology to double back on the past, lingering over the undramatic episode (for example the account of Amelia's sufferings in Brompton), stopping to offer general reflections on human experience, makes for a mood of contemplation rather than galloping excitement. The lengthening perspective permits the slight distancing effect necessary to create the illusion of time passing, so that we take in our stride the information that Dobbin is going grey, or lines are starting to appear on Amelia's forehead, or that Rawdon is too fat for the old Guards uniform he wears when presented at Court (ch. 48), or even the slightly surprising news in chapter 49 that he is 45 years old, although this means he must have aged 15 years in as many chapters.

The impression of time passing is of course an illusion like any other in a novel, and Thackeray evokes it in several ways. The accelerated pace with which he recounts the childhood of young Rawdon and George Osborne has the effect of adding years silently to Becky and Amelia. Then he utilizes the characters' own memories: we see them taking their bearings from past events and in the process becoming aware of the passage of time in their lives. Chief among these events is Waterloo itself, and Thackeray is very skilful at keeping the great battle in our minds throughout the later sections of the novel. It is the fixed point of Amelia's grief, needlessly prolonged by her sentimental idealization of the dead George, and of old Osborne's bitter, confused feelings for his son; and it also marks the start of Dobbin's long frustration, for loyalty to his dead friend prevents him breaking through the shell of sentimentality Amelia has built around the past. There are the little reminders: the relics of the battlefield – 'a pair of French epaulets, a Cross of the Legion of Honour, and the hilt of a sword' (ch. 33) – which Becky sends back to Miss Crawley, Mr Osborne's visit to Brussels and the pompous memorial he causes to be put up in church (ch. 35), Jos's Indian reputation as 'Waterloo Sedley'. These references to Waterloo strengthen our sense of its importance as a turning-point in the characters' lives and in the life of their society. On the far side of Waterloo lie youth and hope; on this the decline into middle age, the loss of illusions, a sobering of style. Of none is this more true than of Rawdon Crawley; it is by our memory of him as a smart officer that we measure the really remarkable change that overtakes him as, eclipsed by Becky, 'the bold and reckless young blood of ten years back was subjugated, and was turned into a torpid, submissive, middle-aged, stout gentleman' (ch. 45). But this change is in keeping with the drift of the novel away from public spectacle into private life and the domestic affections, for Rawdon is altered by his love for his son and his growing affection for his unworldly sister-in-law, Lady Jane. Thackeray manages this change so effectively by dignifying rather than suppressing our sense of the soldier in Rawdon: he becomes the 'Colonel', a 'Waterloo man' (see the illustration in chapter 37, 'Georgy Makes Acquaintance with a Waterloo Man'), and the conjunction of the soldier and the father in him is caught in one brilliant little detail: when Rawdon secretes sweets from Becky's dinners to give to his son, he hides them 'in a certain old epaulet box' (ch. 37).

Waterloo is only the most striking example of a landmark in the past which measures the passage of time for the characters. Reminders of the past are everywhere in *Vanity Fair*, sometimes wilfully cultivated to shut out the present, like the miniature of George Osborne which Amelia keeps always about her, or calculatingly preserved for their future utility as the unsentimental Becky does: it is from her 'little desk' (ch. 53) of mementoes – an ironic contrast to Amelia's sentimental hoardings – that she produces the billet-doux at the end which reveals to Amelia the reality of George's conduct in Brussels. She has also preserved the painting of Jos on the elephant, 'the old picture that used to hang up in Russell Square' (ch. 67), and brings it out at Pumpernickel to ingratiate herself again with Jos and Amelia. Indeed the last section of the novel is thick with the sense of *déjà vu*. When Dobbin returns to London in chapter 58 he goes to stay at the Slaughters': 'Long years had passed since he saw it last. . . . He had now passed into the stage of old-fellow-hood. His hair was grizzled, and many a passion and feeling of his youth had grown grey in that interval.' But the waiter is unchanged, he puts Dobbin in his old room, and recalls 'Captain Osborne': ' "He owes me three pounds at this minute. Look here, I have it in my book. 'April 10, 1815, Captain Osborne: £3.'." ' The reader's memory is being jogged as well as Dobbin's, for it was from the Slaughters' in April 1815 that George and Dobbin left for George's wedding, taking the same road down Piccadilly that Dobbin does now — 'The arch and the Achilles statue were up since he had last been in Piccadilly; a hundred changes had occurred which his eye and mind vaguely noted' (ch. 58).

These continual reminders of the characters' pasts and the changing landscape around them constitute an important part of Thackeray's originality in *Vanity Fair*. No previous novel in the language has this degree of temporal richness and depth, put to such effective use; for the long perspectives which open in the second half of the novel bring home that sense of the transitoriness of pleasure and the erosions of time which lies at the heart of his vision of life. Critics who object to the narrator's reflections on the vanity of human wishes ignore the extent to which Thackeray shows as well as tells, the way he makes us experience the burden of time and change that weighs upon his characters. Take, for example, the account of Amelia's life with her parents in Brompton. This occupies little more than three chapters (38, 46, 50) in the third quarter of the novel, and yet the impression conveyed is of a long, slow capitulation to poverty and care. From the quarrel with her mother over 'Daffy's Elixir' and the never-healed breach it opens up, through the scrimping and saving to buy clothes for Georgy and send him to school, the failure of her father's schemes and Mr Osborne's offer, to the quarrel with her mother over the books she has bought for Georgy with the proceeds from the sale of Dobbin's shawl ('Books, when the whole house wants bread!') and the realization that she cannot win against the solving abundance of her father-in-law's wealth, and must surrender her son to him — in all this nothing is baulked; we are made to feel the gradual unrelenting pressure of genteel poverty which brings Amelia to her knees. Moreover Thackeray's satirical vision of the cruelty of wealth — old Osborne chuckling over Amelia's surrender: ' "Reg'lar starved out, hey? ha, ha! I knew she would" ' (ch. 50) — is strengthened in its turn by the spectacle of Amelia's gradual dispossession and the souring of her home.

Chapter 50 ('Contains a Vulgar Incident') concludes number XIV with a picture of Amelia at what seems the lowest ebb of her fortunes, at last surrendering Georgy to his grandfather. 'No angel has intervened. The child is sacrificed and offered up to fate; and the widow is quite alone.' The contrast between this chapter, which ends with Amelia wandering alone in Russell Square, and chapter 51, in which Becky is seen at the pinnacle of her success at the Gaunt House charades, could hardly seem more absolute, and indeed it brings to a dramatic focus the difference between the silent and often lonely life of the affections, which Amelia, Dobbin, Lady Jane and increasingly Rawdon lead, and the brilliantly lit fairground or theatre where Becky performs. It is appropriate that Becky's moment of triumph should be a theatrical one ('She had reached her culmination: her voice rose trilling and bright over the storm of applause: and soared as high and joyful as her triumph'), for her whole career of fashion has been based upon acting a part. The reader's response to her, too, is shaped in this section of the novel by a developing awareness of what her acting skills involve in moral terms. In the early chapters her talent for mimicry had been an instrument of truth and satire, subversively exposing humbug and social pretension; and it continues to function in this way later, as for example when she imitates Lady Southdown administering her quack medicines:

> Becky acted the whole scene for them. She put on a night-cap and gown. She preached a great sermon in the true serious manner: she lectured on the virtue of the medicine which she pretended to administer, with a gravity of imitation so perfect, that you would have thought it was the Countess's own Roman nose through which she snuffled. 'Give us Lady Southdown and the black dose,' was a constant cry amongst the folks in Becky's little drawing-room in May Fair. And for the first time in her life the Dowager Countess of Southdown was made amusing.
>
> (ch. 41)

But such moments of redeeming comedy become rarer as the novel progresses and Thackeray reveals the price that has to be paid for 'the pursuit of fashion under difficulties' (ch. 37). Living well on nothing a year also involves acting, but of a more desperate and deceitful kind. Perhaps the turning-point in our understanding of Becky comes not in the great exposure scene in chapter 53, but on her presentation at Court and invitation to Gaunt House in chapter 48, when we realize how *necessary* these marks of social recognition have become to her increasingly insubstantial career of fashion. The Becky who looks up the Steyne family names in the Peerage seems no longer the critic of Vanity Fair but its victim. It comes as something of a shock to discover that she is now out of her depth.

So, although Becky's public career of fashion seems − and in many ways is − the antithesis of Amelia's life of silent suffering, our growing sense of its instability, and even of Becky's isolation as she climbs away from Rawdon and all her old friends, makes her too seem vulnerable to the lessons of time and the disappointments it brings. There are other similarities beneath the obvious differences, such as the fact that both heroines have young sons, both are pressed for money, both have a circle of male admirers (the Brompton equivalents of the Gaunt House gallants around Becky are the curate, the doctor, and the old Chevalier de Talonrouge mentioned in chapter 38). Thackeray uses these parallels between genteel and humble life to suggest a deeper congruence between the two girls in their experience of the vanity of human wishes. One must not make this seem too reductive and Thackeray does not, but it is interesting to observe how he brings the long perspective of time to bear on Becky's social triumphs too, and uses it to convey the ephemerality of fashion. A good example is chapter 51 but the whole of number XV (chs. 51–3) is worth looking at from this point of view.

The tone of the chapter is anticipated by the initial drawing in the first edition (see figure 5, p. 60) which shows two men, possibly archaeologists, walking over and examining a giant fallen statue of George IV. This reminds the reader, if he needs reminding at this stage, that Becky's triumph at Gaunt House takes place in the past, not just some vague narrative past but a period, the 1820s, which had become almost 'historical' for people of Thackeray's generation. The suggestion of archaeology is taken up by the narrator at the end of his reflections on fashion in the first paragraph: 'And some day or other (but it will be after our time, thank goodness,) Hyde Park Gardens will be no better known than the celebrated horticultural outskirts of Babylon; and Belgrave Square will be as desolate as Baker Street, or Tadmor in the wilderness.' The narrator then tracks farther back, into the eighteenth century, to recall Baker Street in the days of Pitt and Dundas ('What would not your grandmothers have given to be asked to Lady Hester's parties in that now decayed mansion?'). When we do move forward to the account of Becky's social success it is with our minds coloured by the melancholy of these past vanities, and in the knowledge that Becky's vanities are past also. Like Lady Hester, who 'once lived in Baker Street, and lies asleep in the wilderness', Becky's life of fashion belongs to history, the history of the long dead George IV, so that we approach the brilliant scene itself with a sense of the pathos of time and with the melancholy tones of *Vanitas Vanitatum* echoing in our minds: 'And let us make the best of Becky's aristocratic pleasures likewise – for these too, like all other mortal delights, were but transitory.'

The interaction of 'panorama' and 'scene' (Lubbock's terms), or as I should prefer, retrospect and drama, is most subtle in this and the following chapters. The flow of retrospect enables Thackeray to present a generalized picture of the Steyne era in Becky's life which is shot through with reminders of its pastness and brevity, yet this is combined with the dramatic present tense narration of the charades, and the real — as opposed to artificial — drama with which the chapter ends, when Rawdon, having played Agamemnon to Becky's Clytemnestra in the charade, finds himself a victim in earnest. At this point the reader might expect Thackeray to press on through Rawdon's arrest to the crisis in Becky's affairs, but he chooses instead to interrupt the narrative momentum with another retrospect. Chapter 52 tracks back in time to explain how Lord Steyne has managed to remove Briggs and young Rawdon, the two 'out-sentinels' who guard Becky, and this provides the occasion for a further account of how parenthood has changed Rawdon. His sense of loss when the boy is sent away to boarding-school is surely meant to remind us of Amelia's very similar feelings about Georgy's departure to Russell Square in the previous number, and so to heighten our awareness of the loneliness of the man and the extent to which he has changed in the course of the novel, from the bold dragoon of the pre-Waterloo chapters to the 'poor fellow' who now seeks the company of the gentle, domestic Lady Jane (the Amelia, as it were, of upper-class society). What makes this change so convincing and so moving is Rawdon's inarticulacy about it:

> Rawdon thanked his sister a hundred times, and with an ardour of gratitude which touched and almost alarmed that soft-hearted woman. 'Oh,' said he, in his rude, artless way, 'you — you don't know how I'm changed since I've known you, and — and little Rawdy. I — I'd like to change somehow. You see I want — I want — to be — .' He did not finish the sentence, but she could interpret it. (ch. 53)

By circling back in this way to remind us of the awakened decency in Rawdon, Thackeray strengthens and deepens the effect of the confrontation scene with Becky and Lord Steyne at the end of chapter 53. It has been said that this famous moment in the novel is too 'theatrical' and melodramatic, with the lights blazing, Becky sparkling in adulterous jewellery, the jealous husband confounding the wicked nobleman. There is a certain truth in this criticism if the dramatic scene is considered in isolation, but to do so is to ignore the careful preparation for it. The moral power of the confrontation lies not in individual dramatic gestures, such as the scarring of Steyne's bald forehead with the diamond brooch, but in the clash of values which comes from approaching it through Rawdon and with a sense of the way in which Rawdon is now linked in our minds – by his loneliness, his love for his son, his indifference to fashion – with the novel's decent, unworldly characters, like Dobbin, Amelia and Lady Jane. Nor is it simply the pathos of the 'poor fellow' which persuades us of this. Thackeray has started to call Rawdon 'the Colonel' in these chapters, and as he leaves the spunging-house in his now shabby evening-dress, running through 'the great squares of Vanity Fair' to Curzon Street, it is with the courage and honour of an old soldier that we see him confront and strike Steyne:

> 'You lie, you dog!' said Rawdon. 'You lie, you coward and villain!' And he struck the Peer twice over the face with his open hand, and flung him bleeding to the ground. It was all done before Rebecca could interpose. She stood there trembling before him. She admired her husband, strong, brave, and victorious.

Thackeray told a friend that when he wrote that last sentence, 'I slapped my fist on the table and said "*that* is a touch of genius" '.[4] It is, and what makes it so is not just the surprising insight into Becky's character (she has lost everything and yet can admire the man who is upsetting all her plans), but also the reminder of the origins of their marriage and the source of Rawdon's attraction for her. She is thrilled by this resurrection of the soldier in him, and we may just recall the Becky who went to sleep in the Crawley town house thinking of the red-jacketed soldier in the family picture (ch. 7). And there is another echo which this scene may awaken. The other great climax in *Vanity Fair* is the Brussels number, where, as we saw, fashion and war were brought into dramatic collision. The parallel with that earlier scene seems unmistakable, as Rawdon the 'Waterloo man' destroys the little temple of fashionable vanities Becky has created in May Fair.

> The drawers were all opened and their contents scattered about – dresses and feathers, scarfs and trinkets, a heap of tumbled vanities lying in a wreck. Her hair was falling over her shoulders; her gown was torn where Rawdon had wrenched the brilliants out of it. She heard him go downstairs a few minutes after he left her, and the door slamming and closing on him.

The scene ends with Becky's maid gathering up her trinkets, as the souvenir-hunters had collected mementoes from the field of Waterloo. Significantly perhaps, the next chapter is called 'Sunday after the Battle'.

⁴ James Hannay, *A Brief Memoir of the late Mr Thackeray* (Edinburgh, 1864), pp. 20–1.

4. The Ending and the Narrator

(Monthly numbers XVI–XX, chapters 54–67)

After Becky's downfall much of the steam goes out of the central Amelia/Becky antithesis and, it could be argued, out of the character of Becky herself. She is absent from all of XVII (chs. 57–60) and all but the last chapter of XVIII (chs. 61–3), and when she returns it is not only inevitably diminished in fortune but also, to some extent, in stature as well. 'She rouged regularly now', we are told, 'and her maid got cognac for her besides that which was charged in the hotel bill' (ch. 64). This seems a gratuitous touch, like the clinking of the brandy-bottle on the plate under the bed-cover when she receives Jos in the following chapter, or the hint at the end – more than a hint if we take into account the illustration entitled 'Becky's second appearance in the character of Clytemnestra' – that she has murdered Jos for his insurance policy. It is as if Thackeray had become uncertain about what to do with Becky in the last quarter of the novel, or perhaps uneasy about leaving moral ambiguities unresolved in the minds of his more literal-minded and censorious readers, and had to resort to these melodramatic indications of vice. Drinking, gambling and murder invite easy moral categorization, whereas the whole point about Becky hitherto is that she has been difficult to categorize.

On the other hand Thackeray may have felt that a resurgent Becky would have threatened the equilibrium of the ending he had planned for *Vanity Fair*. The last four numbers belong essentially to the quiet characters, especially to those long-distance winners (if they are winners) Amelia and Dobbin. It is appropriate, too, that the un-nostalgic, forward-looking Becky should be a muted presence in chapters so redolent of time past. I have already suggested that there is an element of deliberate recurrence in such scenes as Dobbin's return to the Slaughters' Coffee House in chapter 58, where the passage of time is emphasized by carefully placed reminders of the characters' past lives and of past action that we, as readers, have witnessed. Another example is the burial of Amelia's mother in the Brompton churchyard, 'upon just such a rainy, dark day, as Amelia recollected when first she had been there to marry

George' (ch. 57). Dobbin and Amelia are especially sensitive to such moments of recall — it is a sign that they alone are capable of learning the lessons of time — but these are frequent towards the end of *Vanity Fair*, and are obviously meant to have structural and thematic importance. Thackeray seems to want us to be aware not just of the characters' pasts but, if one can put it this way, of *our* past as readers of his novel. A fairly obvious example is chapter 56, 'Georgy is made a Gentleman', which shows old Osborne doing his best to turn his grandson into a spoilt, selfish dandy like his son. The fact that he can repeat his original mistakes, without realizing how they contributed to his own sufferings as a parent, reveals that he has learnt nothing from time.

Most of the characters are like Mr Osborne in this respect, and their failure to learn from experience adds a further dimension to the meaning of vanity in the novel. The reader is invited to reflect on these recurrences by the way the closing chapters echo and parallel the opening scenes. The wheel comes full circle for all the main characters at the end. When we meet Becky again at Pumpernickel she has returned to the bohemian society from which she started her social rise: 'Becky liked the life. She was at home with everybody in the place, pedlars, punters, tumblers, students and all' (ch. 65). By taking Becky up and reinstalling her in respectable society, Amelia is repeating the pattern of the early chapters, as is Jos Sedley by allowing himself to fall victim a second time to Becky's flattery. The 'old piano' (ch. 59) and the reappearance of the elephant picture (ch. 67) recall the Russell Square days of Sedley prosperity, while the deaths of old Osborne and Mr Sedley in chapter 61 ('In which Two Lights are put out') prompt the narrator to reflect on the different way fortune has treated the two men — prosperous friends when the novel started and now levelled again in death. Then there are the reminders of Brussels and Waterloo: George's letter found in his dead father's pocket, or the billet-doux produced by Becky in the final chapter.

The point of these echoes and parallels, apart from the symmetry they provide, is to remind us how far we have travelled with the characters, and to give us a sense of the shape of their lives in time. One particularly suggestive instance is Amelia's return to the Osborne house in Russell Square, 'which she had not entered since she was a girl', after Mr Osborne's death. She goes into Georgy's bedroom:

> She went up to one of the open windows (one of those at which she used to gaze with a sick heart when the child was first taken from

her) and thence as she looked out she could see over the trees of Russell Square, the old house in which she herself was born, and where she had passed so many happy days of sacred youth. They all came back to her, the pleasant holidays, the kind faces, the careless, joyful past times; and the long pains and trials that had since cast her down. She thought of these and of the man who had been her constant protector, her good genius, her sole benefactor, her tender and generous friend.

'Look here, mother,' said Georgy, 'here's a G. O. scratched on the glass with a diamond; I never saw it before, I never did it.'

'It was your father's room long before you were born, George,' she said, and she blushed as she kissed the boy.

She was very silent as they drove back to Richmond.

                                                                (ch. 61)

Prospect becomes retrospect and then reflection: as Amelia surveys this landscape of her past the different stages of her life are caught up in memory, and beneath the characteristic Thackerayan poignancy at the passing of time we sense the 'silent' process of reinterpretation going on in Amelia which will bring her in the end to see the value of the constancy, the true gentlemanliness (as opposed to George Osborne's sham dandyism) of Dobbin. The moment is delicately suggestive rather than analytical in its approach to the character's inner life, and the more effective for being so. It is presumably because Amelia is able to grow in understanding in this way, however slowly, to learn the lessons of time, that she and Dobbin and Georgy are the only puppets left standing in the children's puppet-box in the novel's final illustration (see figure 1, p. 55). They alone have been able to rise above the melancholy illusions of Vanity Fair.

Or have they? The path from this moment of Amelia's self-realization to her union with Dobbin at the end is not a straightforward one; it takes in the painful scene in the penultimate chapter when Dobbin at last tells her that she is not worth the love he has given her and that his devotion has been wasted: ' "I knew all along that the prize I had set my life on was not worth the winning; that I was a fool, with fond fancies, too, bartering away my all of truth and ardour against your little feeble remnant of love" ' (ch. 66). And when the moment of romantic reunion comes, on the rainswept Ostend shore, it seems ominously ambiguous:

The vessel is in port. He has got the prize he has been trying for all his life. The bird has come in at last. There it is with its head on his shoulder, billing and cooing close up to his heart, with soft out-stretched fluttering wings. This is what he has asked for every day and hour for eighteen years. This is what he pined after. Here it is – the summit, the end – the last page of the third volume. Good-bye, Colonel. – God bless you, honest William! – Farewell, dear Amelia. – Grow green again, tender little parasite, round the rugged old oak to which you cling!

(ch. 67) ·

Conventional expectations of romantic fulfilment are alternately indulged and mocked. The reader is given a sentimental ending only to find himself manipulated by cliché ('billing and cooing') and by irony ('tender little parasite') into facing the fact that he is, after all, reading a novel, and this is 'the last page of the third volume'. Life is not like fiction, or not like the kind of fiction his reader is accustomed to: that has been Thackeray's point throughout the novel. There are darker echoes here too. If this is Dobbin's 'prize' then we can hardly forget his melancholy statement in the previous chapter that 'I knew all along that the prize I had set my life on was not worth the winning'. Nor is the setting hope-ful: the rain that beats down on Dobbin and Amelia may remind an alert reader of the rain at Mrs Sedley's funeral and the rain that spoilt Amelia's wedding-day. The tone of the ending mimics an upbeat romantic conclu-sion, with Dobbin, Odysseus-like, safely in port after all his trials, but its ambiguity seems to point to the pervasiveness of melancholy and loss, and to bear out Thackeray's stated aim 'to leave everybody dissatisfied and unhappy at the end of the story – we ought all to be with our own and all other stories'.[1]

And yet this is not quite the final word on Amelia and Dobbin. The 'last page of the third volume' may evoke the sentimentalism of the con-ventional three-decker, but the last page of *Vanity Fair* speaks in different, less ambiguous tones – not certainly of romantic happiness, but not of loss either. As Amelia ponders the fact that Dobbin is now fonder of his daughter than of her, the narrator qualifies it with: 'But he never said a word to Amelia that was not kind and gentle; or thought of a want of

<hr>

[1] *Letters* II, p. 423; letter of 3 September 1848. I am indebted here to the fine dis-cussion of this scene in Bruce Redwine, 'The Uses of Memento Mori in *Vanity Fair*', *Studies in English Literature* XVII (1977), pp. 657–72.

hers that he did not try to gratify.' The stress falls on Dobbin's kindness
and thoughtfulness, the chivalry of a true gentleman, and on the possibil-
ity of at least a muted happiness which qualifies, if it does not altogether
contradict, the closing note of *Vanitas Vanitatum*.

It is possible, then, to see Amelia and Dobbin at the end either as the
victims of a final vanity, the vanity of romantic illusions, or as the sober
but moderately happy survivors from the wreckage of vanity. Although I
would argue for the second reading, on the grounds that it fits the actual
'last page' of the novel and is supported by the evidence of the final illustration, an equally strong case can be made out for the first. The truth is
that, whatever view we take, the ending is both low-key and ambiguous,
and it raises in an acute form a question which we have touched on in
passing but not as yet fully confronted: the nature and function of the
narrator's commentary, and its relation to Thackeray's vision of life. One
needs to make an initial distinction here between 'commentary' and
'vision', for although a certain leisurely discursiveness is implicit in
Thackeray's use of the long panoramic perspective, it is a great mistake to
assume that the author and his narrator can be equated. Failure to distin-
guish between them partly accounts for the widespread Victorian view
that Thackeray was a cynic — Ruskin said of him that he 'settled like a
meat-fly on whatever one had got for dinner, and made one sick of it'[2]
— and its modern equivalent, the charge that his view of life is trivial or
superficial. It is also important to bear in mind the essentially *fluctuating*
nature of this dramatized narrator and the variety of tones and attitudes
he commands and exploits. Just as the narrator can move easily from the
long perspective to the dramatic scene, from the panorama of retrospect
to the brief illustrating episode and the telling detail, so the narrator's
tone is continually shifting. There is the long view and melancholy
detachment of the puppeteer who ushers in and closes the novel:

> Ah! *Vanitas Vanitatum!* Which of us is happy in this world? Which of
> us has his desire? or, having it, is satisfied?

This is the concluding note but not necessarily the controlling or author-
itative one. Much more frequent is Thackeray's exploitation, usually for
irony, of the medium range view of the average middle-class reader:

---

[2] *Fors Clavigera* (1871–8), letter 31; in *Works*, ed. E. T. Cook and A.
Wedderburn (39 vols., London: George Allen, 1903–12) XXVII, p. 562.

What a dignity it gives an old lady, that balance at the banker's! How tenderly we look at her faults, if she is a relative (and may every reader have a score of such), what a kind, good-natured old creature we find her!

(ch. 9)

Ladies, what man's love is there that would stand a year's nursing of the object of his affection? Whereas a nurse will stand by you for ten pounds a quarter, and we think her too highly paid.

(ch. 40)

There is the somewhat self-conscious tone of the preacher addressing his 'brother wearers of motley' (ch. 19), and (much more effective in my opinion) the terse reflection attached to passages of vividly realized action or observation:

George's body lay in the pretty burial-ground of Laeken. . . in the unconsecrated corner of the garden, separated by a little hedge from the temples and towns and plantations of flowers and shrubs, under which the Roman Catholic dead repose. It seemed a humiliation to old Osborne to think that his son, an English gentleman, a Captain in the famous British army, should not be found worthy to lie in ground where mere foreigners were buried. Which of us is there can tell how much vanity lurks in our warmest regard for others, and how selfish our love is?

(ch. 35)

Then there is the narrator's continual fencing with the worldly point of view, sometimes ironically endorsing it –

Be cautious then, young ladies; be wary how you engage. Be shy of loving frankly; never tell all you feel, or (a better way still) feel very little.

(ch. 18)

– sometimes sheltering behind its conventional reticences, as in the much-discussed 'siren' passage at the start of chapter 64 ('We must pass over a part of Mrs Rebecca Crawley's biography with that lightness which the world demands'), but always suggesting the limitations of worldliness, its hypocrisy about vice, its heartlessness:

> Have we a right to repeat or to overhear her prayers? These, brother, are secrets, and out of the domain of Vanity Fair, in which our story lies.
>
> (ch. 26)

> There was only Amelia to stand by and support with her gentle arms the tottering, heart-broken, old man. We are not going to write the history; it would be too dreary and stupid. I can see Vanity Fair yawning over it *d'avance*.
>
> (ch. 56)

It is very difficult to generalize about such varying narrative strategies and moods, and that, in a sense, is just the point. Summary descriptions of the author/narrator as the showman of Vanity Fair, or the sentimental cynic (the titles of two critical studies), can only simplify the unsettling dramatic life of a Thackeray novel. Readers used to the relatively fixed narrative distance and consistency of tone in Fielding and George Eliot often see this as a weakness in Thackeray and accuse him, in J. I. M. Stewart's words, of having 'failed to find for himself any constant stance before the human spectacle'.[3] One cannot deny that Thackeray sometimes seems the victim rather than the master of ambiguity, that he tends to oscillate between affirming Amelia's gentleness and mocking her stupidity, or falters when trying to balance his identification with Becky's spirit and his revulsion from her morals (hence perhaps the resort to the rouge-pot and the brandy-bottle at the end). Nor could he resist calling Dobbin a 'spooney' (ch. 66) or pointing out his lisp and yellow face at the very moment of saluting him as the one true gentleman in the novel (ch. 62). A defence of Thackeray from the charge of cynicism or inconsistency might begin by noting that these *unresolved* ambiguities do not bulk very large in our memory of reading the novel and are few in comparison with the many instances of successfully calculated ironies of narrative tone. But such a defence, if it is to be honest, must also go on to admit that a certain irresolution was endemic to his habit of mind. It is not that Thackeray lacked a firm grasp on his satirical targets, vanity and

---

[3] Introduction to *Vanity Fair* (London: Penguin, 1968), p. 22.

selfishness, but that he could not rest in an unequivocal moral position as his great rival Dickens tended to do; his 'peculiar and characteristic scepticism', in Bagehot's phrase, led him on to question even the unworldliness he affirmed against the worldliness he satirized.

This unresting scepticism is the motive-force of *Vanity Fair*, and gives rise to the variety of authorial tones and postures which prevent Thackeray achieving that 'constant stance before the human spectacle' which, on one view, is held to be necessary for the novelist. But it may be argued that Thackeray's scepticism is no less an instrument of truth than the analysis of more consistent moralists − indeed that it helped him to see certain things more clearly than for example Dickens or George Eliot could, with their commitment to Victorian notions of moral nobility and self-sacrifice. He was alert to the other side of the moral coin from that represented by the Little Dorrits and Felix Holts of Victorian fiction − to the selfishness that lurks in Amelia's self-sacrifice, the self-delusion in Dobbin's devotion, the power of poverty to sour and corrupt Mrs Sedley. ' "I think I could be a good woman if I had five thousand a year" ', Becky reflects in a famous passage. 'And who knows but Rebecca was right in her speculations − ', is the narrator's characteristic response, 'and that it was only a question of money and fortune which made the difference between her and an honest woman?' (ch. 41). It is questions like these, probing the bases of the reader's moral assumptions and judgments, which make Thackeray such an 'uncomfortable' writer. When critics accuse him of cynicism what they often seem to mean is that he does not flatter their moral idealism.

Carlyle concluded of Thackeray that 'he had no convictions, after all, except that a man ought to be a gentleman, and ought not to be a snob'.[4] Bagehot put it more charitably, and more perceptively, when he said that 'more than most writers of fiction he felt the difficulty of abstracting his thoughts and imagination from near facts which *would* make themselves felt. The sick wife in the next room, the unpaid baker's bill', and he noted 'his natural tendency to this stern and humble realism'.[5] The scepticism and the 'humble realism' go together: it is because Thackeray could not forget those 'near facts' of ordinary human struggle and tried to make his art faithful to them that he was distrustful of moral absolutism. As to convictions, perhaps Carlyle was right to say that Thackeray's

[4] *Letters* I, p. cix.
[5] *Literary Studies* II, p. 122.

boiled down to the belief that a man ought to be a gentleman, but only if we understand that word in the sense in which it is redefined in *Vanity Fair* through the character of Dobbin. Gentleness, the absence of personal vanity, modesty, patience, chivalry to the weak and, above all, loyalty: as embodied in Dobbin these are not spectacular qualities, but they lie at the heart of Thackeray's ethic. Such modest but real virtues alone make a decent life possible in the world of *Vanity Fair* and mitigate its evils, ensuring the clear-sightedness necessary to escape the toils of greed and vanity, and the constancy to survive the erosions of time.

Appendix: A Note on Thackeray's Illustrations

Each monthly number of *Vanity Fair* carried as its subtitle 'Pen and Pencil Sketches of English Society', advertising the parallel attractions of the illustrations and perhaps attempting to capitalize on Thackeray's already established reputation as an illustrator of his own work. His illustrations for the novel are of three kinds: full-page engraved plates, smaller wood-cut drawings inserted into the text, and illustrated capital letters (pictorial capitals) at the start of each chapter. All 40 plates are reproduced in the Tillotson edition, as well as some of the inserted woodcuts such as the final drawing of the children looking at the puppets in their box (see figure 1). But no modern edition reproduces the pictorial capitals or all

Ah! *Vanitas Vanitatum!* Which of us is happy in this world? Which of us has his desire? or, having it, is satisfied?—Come children, let us shut up the box and the puppets, for our play is played out.

FIGURE 1

the inserted woodcuts, and no edition after the first carries all the illustrative material placed exactly as Thackeray wished.[1] Most readers of the novel today, then, are missing something of the total effect designed by Thackeray: the question is how significant this loss is. Opinion tends to divide between those who argue that the illustrations are functional and an important guide to Thackeray's intentions, and those who see them as largely decorative and so in the last resort dispensable.

Whichever side we may take on that issue, however, there is at least one illustration in *Vanity Fair* which materially affects how we interpret the text, as J. I. M. Stewart points out in his introduction to the Penguin edition. At the end of the novel Dobbin goes to see Jos in Brussels and finds him living in fear of Becky, his financial affairs in a mess. Jos has taken out an insurance policy on his life, and when he dies 'the solicitor of the Insurance Company swore it was the blackest case that had ever come before him' (ch. 67). In the text Becky's possible complicity in his death remains a supposition: the illustration (figure 2) hardens it into an accusation. 'Becky's second appearance in the character of Clytemnestra' shows a terrified Jos pleading with Dobbin, and Becky listening behind a curtain with what looks like a phial of poison in her hand. The analogy with Clytemnestra is underlined, and murder is added to the list of Becky's sins. In many ways this is an unfortunate illustration, unnecessarily coarsening the character of Becky, but any study of Thackeray's *intentions* in *Vanity Fair* must take it into account.

In what ways, then, is the novel enriched by Thackeray's pencil? My own view is that the full-page plates are for the most part decorative and of uneven quality, although they sometimes help to emphasize details in the text (as I have suggested at various points in this study) and no sensible reader would wish to be without them. The illustrations which seem most functional – and most rewarding from an interpretative angle – are the smaller drawings, and in particular the pictorial capitals. As John Harvey suggests, their modest scale may have been congenial to Thackeray, providing the limitations of space his talent needed to work to best effect.[2] Certainly they encouraged a closer alliance between pen and pencil than the larger, more formal and composed engravings. At its

[1] See Joan Stevens, 'Thackeray's *Vanity Fair*', *A Review of English Literature* VI (1965), pp. 19–38.
[2] *Victorian Novelists and their Illustrators* (London: Sidgwick & Jackson, 1970), p. 82.

FIGURE 2

simplest, the pictorial capital is an overture to the chapter which picks out and accentuates a dominant theme or mood. Figure 3 is of this kind: it shows a tall clown bowing with wary mockery to the little strutting figure of Napoleon, while soldiers can be seen through the 'O' of 'Our'. This meeting of the clown and the man of destiny catches well the posture of mocking subservience adopted by Thackeray's comic muse, when his 'surprised story' finds itself 'hanging on to the skirts of history' (ch. 18). A more subtle use of Napoleon can be seen in figure 4, where Becky dressed as Napoleon looks out over the Channel to England. Here Thackeray completes the comic parallel between the social climber and the 'Corsican upstart' which has run throughout the novel. Becky began her social 'campaign' shortly before Napoleon made his return to France, and like him she ends up in exile after her defeat − in her case Boulogne, the favourite haven in Victorian times for bankrupts and other exiles from English respectability (hence the title 'A Vagabond Chapter'). There is another dimension to this vignette, for it deliberately recalls and mocks Benjamin Haydon's many paintings of *Napoleon Musing at St. Helena*, which had become a standing joke in artist circles by the time

CHAPTER XVIII.

WHO PLAYED ON THE PIANO CAPTAIN DOBBIN BOUGHT?

FIGURE 3

UR surprised story now finds itself for a moment among very famous events and personages, and hanging on to the skirts of history. When the eagles of Napoleon Bonaparte, the Corsican upstart, were flying from Provence, where they had perched after a brief sojourn in Elba, and from steeple to steeple until they reached the towers of Notre Dame, I wonder whether the Imperial birds had any eye for a little corner of the parish of Bloomsbury, London, which you might have thought so quiet, that even the whirring and flapping of those mighty wings would pass unobserved there?

"Napoleon has landed at Cannes."

CHAPTER LXIV.

A VAGABOND CHAPTER.

FIGURE 4

WE must pass over a part of Mrs. Rebecca Crawley's biography with that lightness and delicacy which the world demands—the moral world, that has, perhaps, no particular objection to vice, but an insuperable repugnance to hearing vice called by its proper name. There are things we do and know perfectly well in Vanity Fair, though we never speak them: as the Ahrimanians worship the devil, but don't mention him: and a polite public will no more bear to read an authentic description of vice than a truly-refined English or American female will permit the word breeches to be pronounced in her chaste hearing. And yet, Madam, both are walking the world before our faces every day, without much shocking us. If you were to blush

Thackeray was writing *Vanity Fair*.[3] Again, a contemporary 'heroic' stereotype is being undermined.

Figure 5 has already been discussed above (p. 43). The fallen statue of George IV is a companion piece to the illustration of the erect statue which prefaces chapter 48, in which Becky is presented to the King at Court. It represents the fallen idol of fashion, specifically of Regency fashion, for George IV was called 'the First Gentleman in Europe' (ch. 48) and his dandified style is opposed in the novel to the true gentlemanliness of Dobbin. As a fallen idol, too, it anticipates Becky's downfall.

These are only a few examples of the way the pictorial capitals supplement and interpret the text of *Vanity Fair*. It is a pity, to say the least, that modern reprints of the novel do not reproduce them in some form, for they do more than merely embellish the text. Without them, *Vanity Fair*

---

[3] I am indebted for this information to Joan Stevens, 'Thackeray's Pictorial Capitals', *Costerus*, New Series II (1974), pp. 126–8.

CHAPTER LI.

IN WHICH A CHARADE IS ACTED WHICH MAY OR MAY NOT PUZZLE THE READER.

FTER Becky's appearance at my Lord Steyne's private and select parties the claims of that estimable woman as regards fashion, were settled; and some of the very greatest and tallest doors in the metropolis were speedily opened to her—doors so great and tall that the beloved reader and writer hereof may hope in vain to enter at them. Dear brethren, let us tremble before those august portals. I fancy them guarded by grooms of the chamber with flaming silver forks with which they prong all those who have not the right of the *entrée.* They say the honest newspaper-fellow who sits in the hall and takes down the names of the great ones who are admitted to the feasts, dies after a little time. He can't survive the glare of fashion long. It scorches

FIGURE 5

can be made to seem a more magisterial, even in places a more solemn masterpiece than it really is. What the pictorial capitals and some of the inserted woodcuts do is to reinforce the ironic, sceptical, self-mocking side of Thackeray's genius. Like the gargoyles on a cathedral, they are irreverent and unsettling – as befits an 'uncomfortable' writer. It may be appropriate, then, to end with a suitably uncomfortable self-portrait. Figure 6 appeared at the end of chapter 9 in the first edition, and shows Thackeray himself – a very large man in real life – shrunk to the size of a small boy and dressed in jester's costume; the comic mask is off, and the expression on his face is sad and perplexed. The interaction of the two moods, the sadness beneath the comedy, and the fact that both are presented in a comic, self-mocking vignette, come as close as any picture could to capturing the spirit in which Thackeray wrote his 'Novel without a Hero'.

FIGURE 6

Select Bibliography

BIOGRAPHY AND LETTERS

G. N. Ray, *Thackeray: the Uses of Adversity* (London: Oxford University Press, 1955).

G. N. Ray, ed., *The Letters and Private Papers of William Makepeace Thackeray* (4 vols., London: Oxford University Press, 1945–6).

BACKGROUND

W. M. Thackeray, 'The Book of Snobs' and 'Novels by Eminent Hands' in *Contributions to 'Punch'*, vol. VI of *The Biographical Edition of the Works of William Makepeace Thackeray*, 13 vols., (London: Smith, Elder, 1898).

K. Tillotson, *Novels of the Eighteen-Forties* (Oxford: Clarendon Press, 1954).

J. A. Sutherland, *Thackeray at Work* (London: Athlone Press, 1974).

R. Gilmour, *The Idea of the Gentleman in the Victorian Novel* (London: Allen & Unwin, 1981).

CRITICISM

W. Bagehot, 'Sterne and Thackeray', in *Literary Studies* (2 vols., London: Dent, 1911) II, pp. 94–129.

P. Lubbock, *The Craft of Fiction* (London: Cape, 1921).

J. A. Lester, jun., 'Thackeray's Narrative Technique', *PMLA* LXIX (1954), pp. 392–409.

G. Tillotson, *Thackeray the Novelist* (Cambridge: Cambridge University Press, 1954).

K. Tillotson, *Novels of the Eighteen-Forties*

A. E. Dyson, *The Crazy Fabric: Essays in Irony* (London: Macmillan, 1966).

B. Hardy, *The Exposure of Luxury: Radical Themes in Thackeray* (London: Peter Owen, 1972).

J. Carey, *Thackeray: Prodigal Genius* (London: Faber, 1977).

ILLUSTRATIONS

J. Stevens, 'Thackeray's *Vanity Fair*', *A Review of English Literature* VI (1965), pp. 19–38.

J. Stevens, *Vanity Fair* and the London Skyline', *Costerus*, New Series II (1974), pp. 13–41.

T. T. Gneiting, 'The Pencil's Role in *Vanity Fair*', *Huntington Library Quarterly* XXIX (1976), pp. 171–202.

Index